MICROCULTURES

Understanding the Consumer Forces that
Will Shape the Future of Your Business

Ujwal Arkalgud and
Jason Partridge

ISBN: 978-1-6847-1765-1 (sc)
ISBN: 978-1-6847-1648-7 (hc)
ISBN: 978-1-6847-1647-0 (e)

Library of Congress Control Number: 2019921277

Lulu Publishing Services rev. date: 01/16/2020

TABLE OF CONTENTS

Making a Case for a Consumer-Led Approach to Business

This is not a book. It is a wake-up call. If your business is not taking a consumer-led approach, your days are numbered. Why should you believe us? Collectively, we bring more than thirty-five years' experience working with some of the largest companies and brands in the world. We've worked for these companies in a variety of roles—across advertising, marketing, market research, innovation and business consulting. When we finally decided to start our company more than four years ago, we had a single vision: to become a catalyst for transformation. Based on our last estimate, our front-end innovation work has served as the building blocks for more than a hundred net new products and generated more than $5.9 billion in net new revenue in the consumer packaged goods, retail, beauty and beverage marketplace. We are the guys the Chief Technology Officer calls when they have a question no one else can answer. We are the guys the Chief Innovation Officer calls when they need to improve their batting average.

More specifically, we are the guys you call when an organization needs to transform itself, move away from taking a typical, industry-led approach and evolve to take a more empathetic, consumer-led approach. It is this work, where we have taught organizations to properly embrace their consumer, that has inspired us to write our second book. **We call it *Microcultures.***

But before we talk about microcultures, we need to level set. First, most companies are industry-led rather than consumer-led. They define their businesses according to internal or industry created terms, definitions and constructs. For example, a food company may say its business is divided into its "shelf-stable" and "refrigerated" grocery business, as well as its new and emerging direct-to-consumer delivery business. Next, it may divide its shelf-stable business into breakfast foods and snacks and its refrigerated business into breakfast foods, snacks and meals. Further, in quarterly and annual reports, the company may call out strategic imperatives to launch what they consider to be "healthy yet convenient" versions of their well-established products to add to the consumer's sense of choice.

This is what we call an industry-led perspective.

Why? Consider the term "shelf stable" for a second. It is completely and utterly meaningless to almost every single one of the food company's consumers. Instead, these consumers use terms like "packaged food" and "boxed food" to refer to what the industry calls "shelf stable." The same is true of the term "healthy." There are more than five major definitions of what healthy means to people. That is, there are more than five microcultures that define what healthy means today in the context of shelf-stable foods (more on this in Chapter One, of course).

Here are two simple examples.

Microculture 1: Healthy shelf-stable foods should be as unaltered as possible, as natural as possible, with the shortest supply chain possible.

Microculture 2: Healthy shelf-stable foods are products that will not "make me fat."

Adding to the complexity is the issue of context. If you change the context of the business from shelf stable to refrigerated, the term "healthy" occupies completely different meanings and different mental models in the minds of consumers today. In a consumer-led context—unlike in an industry-led approach—things are rarely black and white.

Another glaringly obvious example: if you look at any of McDonald's annual reports or Letters to Shareholders, you'll notice the repeated use of the word "restaurant" in describing McDonald's business. This is another classic, industry-led trap. Another commonly used industry term to refer to McDonald's business is QSR, which stands for Quick Service Restaurant. From the consumer's lens, it's a very different story. The consumer may look at McDonald's as a *fast food joint*, a *burger joint*, a *local hang*, or more. But "restaurant" appears nowhere in consumer-led culture.

So, why does the consumer-led perspective matter?

Typically, this kind of perspective and thinking has mattered to middle and upper management (senior managers, directors, vice presidents) but not to the C-Suite. This is because middle management is usually the one tasked with the responsibility of identifying and operationalizing new revenue opportunities. We've been in enough meetings to know that ideas rarely come from the top. Instead, they're typically the domain of middle and upper management. Yes, final sign-off may be the domain of the C-Suite, but the idea and the process of valuing the idea comes from the middle and moves to the top. And therein lies the problem.

If middle and upper management are mandated to think with an industry-led perspective, then everything they do—even if it is done through a consumer-led lens—needs translation in order to flow back up the chain. This not only slows down the process of innovation but, most importantly, waters down ideas and opportunities, resulting in innovations that are nothing but minor changes to packaging, formulation or—worse yet—aesthetics. At least if such incremental innovations worked, we'd have something to show for the trouble. But they don't, more than 80% of the time.

That is why we're writing this book.

When the C-Suite builds strategic mandates, typically with the help of management consultants, they almost always use an industry-led lens. For the record, in the process of writing this book, we talked to more than two hundred executives across the Fortune 1000. Not a single one of their companies used a consumer-led lens. This means that, in order to operationalize the strategy that the C-Suite delivers, senior management builds accountability metrics that are also all industry-led. This ultimately boxes in middle management and prevents any real consumer-led initiatives from taking flight.

Here's a real example from a food company we currently work with in the area of protein. In the past, the C-Suite approached strategic initiatives through the same industry-led lens. This meant that when alternative forms of protein began to emerge on the scene (like those that are plant-derived), they immediately instituted a division dedicated not just to alternative proteins, but to plant-based proteins specifically. This new business division made investments in plant-based technologies and companies and even introduced a new line of products into the marketplace.

Nowhere along the way did senior management ask what the consumer's perspective toward protein really was and whether and how it was evolving.

If they had, they would have realized that the emerging opportunity in the area was actually one around the quality of proteins and around the net nutritional value delivered (it's a cost/benefit analysis that more and more consumers are innately doing in their minds). If the C-Suite had taken a consumer-led approach to their business, they would have constituted a team that focuses on quality and nutrition instead of on plant-based proteins as the solution. Not only would this have opened the door to new innovations that their competitors weren't thinking about, but it would have also prevented excessive investments in areas that just aren't yielding the results desired. Again, the real problem in a scenario like this is that once you've made the decision to undertake a set of heavy industry-led initiatives, middle management has to constantly try and find ways to fit consumer-led perspectives (that they normally work with) into those predefined industry lenses. It's like constantly needing to put a square peg into a round hole. It just never works and eventually ends up wasting time and resources, with very few wins to make up for the effort.

In the four years since we started our research technology firm, which is focused on bringing this consumer-led perspective to innovation initiatives, not a month has gone by where we haven't been asked by middle and senior management to help reshape opportunities into predefined industry perspectives that the C-Suite would understand and approve of. Failing to do so, we're told, will just result in the shelving of an opportunity, no matter how compelling the data might say it is.

This is why this book is for senior leaders, and the C-Suite in particular. We need CTOs, CMOs, CIOs and CEOs to read this so they can understand the inadvertent impact of their decisions to rely on traditional methods of market definition. Just to be clear, there's also plenty of operational frameworks in this book to help middle management bring the concept of microcultures to life. But all that is useless if this book does not land in the hands of the current and future leaders of companies. This book is about transformation. It's about helping senior leaders transform their companies from industry-led businesses to businesses that are consumer-led and empathetic.

Thinking CapEx, not OpEx

So how does one take the idea of being consumer-led and ingrain it into the fabric of an organization from the top down? It starts with a very important financial decision: to make the initial set of transformation projects a capital expenditure. This helps ensure that senior and middle management isn't worried about their budgets and about the short-term operational impact this transformation will inevitably have on their existing initiatives. Furthermore, it gives the doers (middle management in particular) the freedom to experiment and push the envelope of what's possible. It allows them to truly take a consumer-led perspective to not just identify new revenue opportunities but also operationalize those ideas across their and their colleagues' business units. The second half of this book will address the gory details that middle and senior management will need in order to begin to integrate the microcultures lens into their business units and day-to-day operational frameworks.

Another important top-down initiative that only the C-Suite can drive is that of agile thinking. We've all heard about agile frameworks, especially as they are applied to the world of software development. But increasingly, the same methodology is being applied to the structure of companies in order to enable growth and improve innovation success. Taking a consumer-led perspective requires the organization to embrace agile thinking, primarily because the rate of market development and change in consumer culture is staggering in today's hyperconnected digital world. What is meaningful to a set of consumers today will evolve in twelve to eighteen months. Take the simple example of an industry-defined skincare category such as serum. From the industry's perspective, it means something very specific—enhancing one's skin or addressing specific skin problems like aging, blemishes, oil secretion, etc. From the consumer's lens, it means something completely different. It used to be about luxury (having the time and money to go beyond the necessary prerequisites for one's skin). But as the culture of serum evolved, that definition changed in just over 12 months. It increasingly became about preventing the need for makeup or helping minimize the use of makeup products in one's daily ritual. The rate of change in the consumer-led perspective around serum is not just fascinating; it's downright scary. If organizations in the beauty landscape aren't equipped with the agility needed to adapt, they will increasingly find themselves under attack from smaller, more agile start-ups and even foreign competitors. This book therefore addresses this rate of change and explains how the microcultures framework provides organizations with a toolkit they can use to always look ahead instead of reacting once it's too late. This framework will also create an innate openness to agile thinking, because it will make middle and senior management highly aware of the smaller threats that are gradually picking up steam well before they become a reality.

Lastly, this book will help the 99% of us that aren't blessed with the kind of vision that certain leaders like Steve Jobs are innately bestowed with. We can't all just rely on our gut to make decisions. We need the right tools so we can extract the maximum value from our teams and the smartest individuals that work for us. In this way, we can make informed decisions that will drive repeatable success for the entire organization. Most importantly, these decisions will help bring down the abysmal failure rate of corporate innovations. This is why we're so excited for you to read this book.

PART ONE

Understanding Microcultures

CHAPTER ONE

What Is a Microculture?

Culture evolves over time. This we know to be true. Look no further than the changes in meaning we associate with everything from brands to products to images to ideas. Look at the person you were ten years ago and what you believed versus the person you are today. Age is not entirely responsible for changing your worldview or your perspective. It is also the world around you, which has shifted and evolved.

Our job as researchers, innovators, brand champions and lovers of insight is not only to understand this. Our job is to have the foresight to anticipate where culture is going. But this is harder than ever, as we live and work in a world where cultures are transitioning, mutating or being absorbed and reimagined at a rate that is faster than ever before. For proof, look no further than the recent shift in meanings driven by an incident involving the mistreatment of dairy cattle.

How Microcultures Drive Industry

On June 4, 2019, a three-minute video was released on YouTube and Facebook that quickly took the Internet by storm. The video, which showed graphic footage of dairy cows and newborn calves being cruelly mistreated, had been secretly recorded at the largest dairy farm in the US. Its name was Fair Oaks Farm. It was quickly identified that Fair Oaks was the flagship farm of Fairlife milk, an ultra-filtered milk product owned by the Coca-Cola Company.

A member of the Animal Recovery Mission (ARM), a nonprofit animal rights group, had infiltrated Fair Oaks for three months and had secretly documented numerous incidents of animal abuse. Workers were caught in the act of punching, stabbing and stepping on calves as well as callously hurling them onto trucks or violently kicking them into cages. To reinforce the gravity of the situation, the video featured a voiceover from ARM founder Richard Couto, who explained that in the ten years of the organization's undercover operations, "we have never seen such consistent constant abuse to a newborn baby animal."[1]

Comparisons to concentration camps were made both by the video's narrator and by commenters, who quickly shared the content across their favorite social platforms.

Within hours, the video had gathered millions of views. Within days, grocery stores across the US started pulling Fairlife milk off their shelves. The footage prompted protests across the country, with many animal rights groups calling for a complete industry boycott of the product.[2] Now, the company is facing several class action lawsuits.[3]

The morality of animal welfare aside, this cultural shift in the meanings created and shared by consumers demands our attention. For, if we turn back the clock and examine what the Fairlife culture

[1] Animal Recovery Mission, "The Biggest Undercover Dairy Investigation in History - Fair Oaks Farms and Coca Cola," Facebook video, accessed June 25, 2019, https://www.facebook.com/watch/?v=366221877572310.

[2] Michelle Gant, "Fairlife Dairy Products Pulled from Store Shelves amid Animal Abuse Controversy,"
Today, June 7, 2019, https://www.today.com/food/fairlife-dairy-products-pulled-store-shelves-amid-animal-cruelty-controversy-t155783.

[3] Elaine Watson, "Fairlife, Coca-Cola, Hit with Second Wave of Lawsuits over Animal Abuse Allegations," FoodNavigator-USA, June 20, 2019, https://www.foodnavigator-usa.com/Article/2019/06/20/Fairlife-Coca-Cola-hit-with-second-wave-of-lawsuits-over-animal-abuse-allegations.

stood for only days before the release of this footage, we will see a drastically different story of what the product meant in the mind of the consumer.

When Fairlife milk was first introduced to the US market in December 2014, it celebrated near-instant success. Within its first two years, the product was being sold at 76,000 outlets across the country, and its dollar sales grew by 79%.[4] The brand and product had successfully tapped into consumers' rising concerns around the high sugar content of milk and the human body's ability to digest dairy. Using a high filtration process, Fairlife delivers lactose-free milk that contains 50% more protein, 30% more calcium and 50% less sugar than traditionally produced cow's milk. As a result, consumers accepted and believed in the motto that the company used for the brand.

It truly was, "Milk, only better."[5]

As awareness of the product grew and more consumers learned about the benefits that the brand offered, Fairlife milk carved out a point of differentiation in the marketplace, where it challenged some of the conventional and tired tropes that were still attached to traditional milk. Fairlife was a more progressive and futuristic version of dairy—one that could respond to the consumer's desire for taste and function while simultaneously resolving a lot of the health concerns that were creating anxiety.

Fairlife had tapped into a powerful and influential microculture that was changing the face of dairy. It was perfectly positioned for a group of consumers who prided themselves on spending more money on milk and other dairy products that offered better health, better nutrition, better digestion and—most importantly—tolerability (dairy that's easier to digest).

This brand wasn't just in the right place at the right time. It was in the hands of the right consumer, who was setting the tone and

---

[4] Elaine Watson, "Fairlife Ultra-Filtered Milk Sales Surged 79% in 2016; Core Power and Yup! to Be Brought under Fairlife Brand Umbrella," *FoodNavigator-USA*, September 12, 2017, https://www.foodnavigator-usa.com/Article/2017/09/12/fairlife-ultra-filtered-milk-sales-surged-79-in-2016.

[5] Watson, "Fairlife Ultra-Filtered Milk Sales Surged 79% in 2016."

narrative for what the product represented and stood for. This was a movement in milk culture and it was putting tremendous pressure on the traditional dairy industry.

Then, the Fair Oaks Farm video surfaced. Everything that Fairlife represented changed overnight. The microculture that championed Fairlife milk for its nutrition and tolerability was replaced by another microculture, dedicated to animal welfare.

Why is this so critical?

Because microcultures are the forces in the present that shape the behavior of the mainstream in the future.
Let's unpack this.

A microculture refers to the nuanced and particular sets of meanings that substantially sized groups of the most dominant consumers attribute to an idea, trend or topic at any given point in time. It then in turn gives direction to—and indicates the broader shifts that will happen in—the marketplace and impacts the mainstream (or macroculture).

A microculture is different from a niche group of consumers like the Innovators or the Early Adopters on the Everett Rogers diffusion-of-innovation curve that some of us may be familiar with.

Microcultures are created by large groups of people (numbering into the hundreds of thousands, if not millions) who are engaged in (the largely unconscious process of) justifying or rationalizing their behavior as they seek to amass symbolic capital. This is another way of saying that microcultures create new alibis and justifications that people use for making decisions in order to gain power, status, prestige and acceptance in a particular community or beyond.

Microcultures are powerful because they share a consistent set of beliefs and values that challenge the conventional or mainstream category or movement. In the process of developing, the microculture comes to designate specific forms of symbolic capital. For example, the initial microculture that surrounded the Fairlife brand was shaped based on the symbolic capital that came with challenging norms around conventional dairy. There was cachet in supporting a new, healthier and more tolerable version of milk.

But when the Fair Oaks Farm video went public, it resulted in the growth of another microculture—one anchored to the morality of animal welfare—that had, until then, sat on the sidelines. With its definition promptly tied to a new form of symbolic capital (social prestige is now gained by caring for the animals that provide us with our nourishment and by holding corporate culture accountable for its actions), this microculture instantly reconfigured the meanings associated not just with the Fairlife brand but also with the dairy category in its entirety. This now prominent microculture competes with the older microculture of tolerability and health and creates a new form of symbolic capital (caring for animals) that now sits in tension with the old form.

This book introduces the concept of consumer microcultures for two reasons: first, to explain the dynamism of today's marketplace (caused by the proliferation of digital technologies and new forms of communication, discussed below) and second, to show how the marketplace consists of numerous and interrelated fields of opportunity for companies big and small. By delving into the powerful notion of microcultures, this book tells businesses how they can make sense of new trends and identify revenue opportunities early so they can successfully innovate in the marketplace.

In order to understand the concept of microcultures, it is necessary to take a few steps back to first consider the marketplace as a whole, which is made up of macrocultures (established norms maintained and espoused by mainstream consumers) and microcultures (emerging ideas created and popularized by "lead consumers," or those who create culture). These microcultures typically compete with each other for the legitimization of their preferred forms of symbolic capital and drive a potential shift in the overall marketplace as a result. Consequently, when companies ignore microcultures or fail to track their emergence, influence, trajectory and growth, they leave themselves vulnerable to the competition and miss opportunities for business growth.

This is why research, insight and foresight are increasingly important among the Fortune 1000. Thanks to technological advancements and global shifts in economic power (and population), not to mention the increasingly critical, intelligent and evolving consumer, there is tremendous disruption in the marketplace. Insight can no longer rest on its laurels or make billion-dollar bets on focus group verbatims from dangerously low sample sets. Instead, research and insight teams are pressed to deliver more accurate predictions based on data-driven studies with shorter turnaround times and smaller budgets.

This is the future of the market research industry: embracing new technologies like artificial intelligence and machine learning to make observational research on demand.

The companies that will thrive will be the ones that employ researchers who embrace new technologies to streamline and automate old practices, learn more from data collection and analysis and refocus the team's time to concentrate on higher-level problem-solving and prototyping.

Identifying, sizing, decoding and eventually tailoring solutions to microcultures will be key to helping research achieve the accurate yet fast answers the C-Suite requires to make their innovation bets. And, as you will learn in this book, these practices will help your organization uncover the detail needed to quickly and succinctly deliver ethnographic insights. Our argument is that when it comes to identifying the up-and-coming shift that will drive change in the market, *the microculture of today will evolve to become the macroculture of tomorrow.* This sets the tone for how we can anticipate where the remainder of an industry is going next. The focus over the next few chapters is going to be on understanding, recognizing and valuing these microcultures so that we can better identify revenue opportunities that have growth potential.

But before we talk about the impact microcultures will have on insight teams in the future, let's take a moment to consider some of the challenges that insight teams wrestle with today. After all, these challenges largely explain why, despite so much time and effort, innovation teams fail at such an alarming rate.

One of the most dominant challenges we have seen is companies being mesmerized by an "industry perspective" that is typically at odds with—or even inaccurate when compared to—the "consumer perspective." An industry-led perspective is commonly what is talked about in syndicated trend reports and consequently in the popular press. It is also often what everyone in an organization is talking about. Needless to say, an industry perspective is also a popular perspective. But the allure of popularity puts us at risk of parity, that is, where our product or solution is not differentiated in the mind of the consumer. And an industry perspective can often skew our understanding of what is truly relevant to consumers.

The Industry Reality is Rarely the Consumer Reality

Let's look at an example from the US skincare industry to further highlight why this distinction between an industry- and a consumer-led perspective is so important, and how microcultures can help us keep it in mind.

In late 2018, a major cosmetics brand was getting ready to launch a line of "natural products" after spending eighteen months investing in R&D and consumer research (focus groups, interviews, cocreation sessions, etc.) to "get it right."

What they learned from their research was that when it came to natural skincare, consumers reported being interested in nontoxic organic ingredients that were kinder to the environment and the skin. Before committing the tens of millions of dollars it would take to implement this new line, they hired us to analyze the product's revenue opportunities and identify relevant demand spaces—i.e., pinpoint growth opportunities by identifying how different types of people satisfy different types of needs on different types of occasions. To put it simply, a demand space is an insight that clearly defines your market, shows the opportunities you can harness for growth, and tells you how to go about this.[6]

After just five days of research looking at the topic through the lens of microcultures, we had determined that the nuanced meanings

---

[6] Nic Bulois, "Greater Insight: Spot the Demand Space to Find Your Path to Growth," *Campaign*, July 22, 2013, https://www.campaignlive.co.uk/article/greater-insight-spot-demand-space-find-path-growth/1192614?src_site=marketingmagazine.

that large numbers of consumers assign to the topic of "natural" in the context of skincare were not in line with what the company had initially assumed. We found that consumers were no longer trusting claims of "natural ingredients" or "all-natural" products; the industry had already overdone it, and "natural" was no longer a demand space with growth potential. The only opportunity for growth within "natural" was in the area of biologically active ingredients (derived from nature). Interestingly, the overall product didn't need to be "natural" if such ingredients made their way into the product line. In short, the microculture of natural products was already on its way out and being replaced with a microculture of biologically active ingredients. New meanings around biologically active ingredients were thus exerting pressure on the previously dominant microculture of natural ingredients that had surrounded the topic of skincare.

It is precisely this shift in meaning that our client had to consider in order to maximize revenue opportunities. Had they gone with their original, industry-led assumption that "natural" occupied a lucrative space, their product would have ended up like one of the thousands of product lines that fail when they are brought to market. By contrast, the consumer perspective that we were able to identify by analyzing the microcultures around skincare showed us instead that "natural" didn't have much left to offer the marketplace and that it was in fact associated with unreliable and rather distorted information. Which brings us to the question of why microcultures are especially important in today's business landscape where, despite incredible improvements in how we design and bring new products to life, the failure rate of innovation has not reduced one bit.

Let's look at another example of an industry-led innovation that relied too heavily on misplaced assumptions about new revenue opportunities, this time by examining the now classic case study of a failed innovation: Segway.

A motorized personal transportation vehicle, Segway was introduced to the market in 2001. The company behind Segway (and many other market forecasters) believed that it would revolutionize how people move across cities; the urban masses would surely favor the fuel-efficient Segway over cars, motorcycles, bicycles or public

design thinking process in their own operations.[13] While this has led to the development of more beautifully designed and high-performing products, it hasn't helped reduce the 80 to 95% failure rate of business innovation. So what is happening? Despite this shift in thinking and investment by the corporate world, why do we continue to see such a high rate of failure?

Because too many companies look at the design thinking process as the first step in innovating when it should be the second step. To properly prepare to innovate, one must first identify new opportunity areas, map them, and assign a value to them. This is where a company identifies a particular opportunity space as being lucrative enough to justify investing time, effort and, most importantly, money.

Imagine you are a traditional yogurt manufacturer. You are looking at where shifts in culture are emerging that may yield opportunity, and you may decide that the area most likely to drive growth is not just plant-based products but specifically the context of nutritionally fortified foods (a plant-based product that doesn't leave me lacking nutritionally). Once the opportunity space is identified, the next part of the innovation process is the product design work. This is where the traditional yogurt manufacturer would do cocreation sessions with the consumer to distill initial ideas down to specific opportunities, develop prototypes, retest and validate and go to launch.

But imagine our yogurt manufacturer again. Imagine that they understand that there is an increasing interest in plant-based options in the market, but they do not spend the time to clearly outline and understand the opportunity area. As they look to work directly with consumers in their interviews or cocreation sessions, the consumer is unaware of or unable to articulate their anxiety around nutrition.

---

[13] Rikke Dam and Teo Siang, "What is Design Thinking and Why is it So Popular?" *Interaction Design Foundation*, September 2019, https://www.interaction-design. org/literature/article/what-is-design-thinking-and-why-is-it-so-popular; see also Lohr, "IBM's Design-Centered Strategy 2015"; YoungJoong Chang, Jaibeom Kim, and Jaewoo Joo, "An Exploratory Study on the Evolution of Design Thinking: Comparison of Apple and Samsung," *Design Management Journal* 8, no. 1 (2013): 22–34.

Instead, they use alibis like health, wellness or environmental sustainability as the reasons they are gravitating toward plant-based solutions.

The design thinking process reminds us of the game "broken telephone." In the game, players must stand in a straight line. The first person whispers a word or phrase into the ear of the person standing to their right, and the game continues until it reaches the end of the line. The last player says the phrase out loud so everyone can hear how much it has changed from the first whisper at the beginning of the line.

Now, imagine that instead of a phrase being shared, the first player is sharing a "human truth." As the human truth is shared, we learn more about what it means to different people, and thus we begin to understand the needs of the many. These needs can inform emotional and effective design for people at a human level. The job of a design thinking team is to strive to eliminate as much confusion and miscommunication as possible, and if a new insight is identified, to go back in the process (or back in the line) to try and make sure that the human truth is never lost and is hopefully transformed into something incredible. But it has to begin with a human truth. It has to begin with something that is grounded.

Jumping to design thinking before identifying opportunity areas is like skipping the first person in the line. Instead, you ask the second person to guess what the first person is thinking. It is a huge leap, without the necessary context.

This is an industry trend we are looking to challenge. And this is why we educate clients to reexamine and rethink the importance of identifying opportunity spaces. Because design thinking is powerful, but only when built on a sturdy foundation.

Are there exceptions to the rule? Of course. Sometimes there is a need for innovation when a perfectly good solution already exists but has some operational flaws and inefficiencies that improved design (the second part of innovation) can resolve. Like a classic innovation case study where, in 2012, GE helped calm children's fears when they had to lie motionless in an MRI scanner. By teaming up with industrial designer Doug Dietz, they created the *MR Adventure Discovery Series* and introduced colorfully decorated scanners and themed imaging rooms in order to make the sterile and off-putting hospital environment less intimidating to young patients.[14] In the "Cozy Camp Experience," children are told that they are being scanned in a special sleeping bag, under a starry sky in a magical camp setting—details that are playfully depicted in the design of the scanner and the examination room and complemented by a story that is integrated into the scanning process, the specific commands that technicians have to communicate to the patient, the machine's loud whirring noises, etc. The effect of transforming a frightening experience for children by reimagining the design of the product in question has significantly reduced scanning times, the rate at which scans have to be redone due to inaccurate readings and the number of children who need to be sedated in order to get the imaging test done.[15]

As heartwarming as this example is, the goal of the project was not to anticipate the next big thing. The goal was to simply solve an existing design problem with the machine. So, the direct application of design thinking models worked. Whereas in situations where a net new revenue opportunity needs to be identified, improvements in empathetic design and human understanding are not enough. We need to know where the real opportunity area lies and what fruit it may yield. And what we have noticed again and again is that the innovation industry has been so busy focusing on improving how they design and market products, it has overlooked how it can get better at identifying the right opportunities to begin with.

It's unfair to say that Segway failed because it was a badly designed product. It failed because it didn't understand what opportunity space it was operating in. And it failed at identifying the opportunity space because it didn't find out what consumers *really* want and need. Let's look at this more closely, as it is a key part of the innovation equation. In

---

[14] General Electric (GE) Healthcare, "From Terrifying to Terrific: The Creative Journey of the Adventure Series," *The Pulse*, accessed June 26, 2019, http://newsroom.gehealthcare.com/from-terrifying-to-terrific-creative -journey-of-the-adventure-series/.
[15] Eyal Alony, "The Adventure Series Makes an MRI Fun for Kids," *Parentology*, May 20, 2019, https://parentology.com/the-adventure-series-makes-mri-fun-for-kids/.

the past and still to this day, companies rely heavily on trend reporting and other types of self-reported industry data and surveys to identify new revenue opportunities for their businesses. Typically, once a trend is identified, a company will then talk to more consumers to see how that trend relates to them. In essence, decisions during the first part of the innovation process happen mostly by asking people about what they need or want in a product or solution. In fact, even most trend reports are created through street-level consumer intercepts and Q&A. This is, of course, problematic, because self-reporting and other interview-based data sources are prone to what psychologists call social desirability bias, a response bias whereby people answer questions in a way that makes them appear favorable to others.[16] This kind of data is also fundamentally biased because consumers' motivations and the meanings they associate with their choices are virtually impossible for them to recognize, let alone articulate in an interview setting because they are so deeply ingrained in their mode of being.[17] A real-life example will clearly illustrate this point.

A good friend of ours recently lost 20 lbs. As she was losing the weight, she talked about being on a cleanse, rather than on a diet. Why? Because "diet" would suggest that she is concerned about conventional norms around body image, something that would undermine her in front of her circle of strong female friends and possibly even herself. A cleanse, by contrast, means that she's someone who is involved in self-care; she's shedding her toxins and taking care of herself. This is an example of the nuanced and hidden meanings created in a

---

[16] Allen Edwards, "The Relationship Between the Judged Desirability of a Trait and the Probability That the Trait Will be Endorsed," *Journal of Applied Psychology* 37, no. 2 (1953): 90–93.

[17] Ryan T. Howell, "Should Marketers Trust Consumer Self-Reports? Marketers Should Think Twice about Trusting Data from Focus Groups," *Psychology Today*, October 23, 2013, https://www.psychologytoday.com/us/blog/cant-buy-happiness/201310/should-marketers-trust-consumer-self-reports; Daniel Kahneman, *Thinking Fast and Slow* (New York: Farrar, Straus and Giroux, 2011); Robert A. Hansen and Carol A. Scott, "Alternative Approaches to Assessing the Quality of Self Report Data," in *Advances in Consumer Research*, vol. 5, ed. Kent Hunt (Ann Arbor, MI: Association for Consumer Research, 1978), 99–102. See also Chapter Two for further elaboration on this point.

microculture around diet versus cleanse, even though the outcome is the same—the loss of 20 lbs. It is more than likely that our friend would not have been able to explain why she chose to say cleanse instead of diet. But the meanings she attributed to her actions through her use of language reveal something very significant about her attitudes and beliefs, and also about the symbolic capital that defines the world she moves in. In other words, in the broader industry or macroculture of health and well-being, dieting is a microculture that is being pressured and changed by a newer microculture of "cleansing," which in turn is changing the symbolic capital that consumers assign to the act of weight loss. For our friend to feel that she fits into her group of strong female friends, this is the symbolic capital she needs to exhibit and strive for. And for innovation professionals, this kind of nuanced information is invaluable as they try to make sense of the intricacies of consumer behavior.

Traditional forms of research—consumer intercepts on the street, interviews, surveys, focus groups—cannot capture these nuances. However, as mentioned, these methods have not changed in decades, although design techniques and innovation strategies have. Companies may leverage hundreds of technologies to design and prototype new products, but they fail to identify ways to improve the first part of innovation: the process that identifies the nuanced meanings that are continuously created by consumers and that indicate where the marketplace is headed and, thus, where new revenue opportunities lie.

In order to understand how we can improve this first part of innovation, we need to start by understanding a few things about the world we currently live in—specifically, the digital revolution that defines it. Going back to the Fairlife milk scandal, for example, we not only see how it illustrates shifts in microculture and how these shifts can forecast market success (or indicate failure), but also how tremendous the influence of Internet connectivity and social media (YouTube and Facebook in this case) is and how instantaneously meanings around a product or an industry can change as a result. Let us examine this in more detail.

Companies' failure to accurately identify revenue opportunities before it's too late is, by and large, symptomatic of a broader phenomenon that defines our digital age: the unprecedented access to information and the staggering speed and volume of online communication. For example, there are more than 3.9 billion Internet users worldwide, with North America accounting for 14% of these.[18] Social media use is also pervasive, with an estimated worldwide user rate of approximately 2.77 billion in 2019, up from 2.46 billion in 2017 across all age groups.[19] The everyday lives of consumers in the connected world are thus significantly impacted by daily Internet usage.[20]

One major effect of this unprecedented volume of online interaction and communication is a nonstop proliferation of ideas, practices and meanings by consumers in the marketplace.[21] As a result, consumers are creating marketplaces at an unprecedented rate; marketplaces that are nothing but unique combinations of meanings. And the corporate world is struggling to keep up.

But how do we get at and understand the nuances of these ever-changing and burgeoning meanings? **We need to rethink how we do research.** Traditional methods of product and trend research, as

---

[18] J. Clement, "Number of Internet Users Worldwide 2005–2018," *Statista*, January 9, 2019, https://www.statista.com/statistics/273018/number-of-internet-users-worldwide/.

[19] North America ranks first among regions where social media is highly popular, with a social media penetration rate of 66%. In 2016, more than 81% of the United States population had a social media profile. As of the second quarter of 2016, US users spend more than 215 weekly minutes on social media via smartphone, 61 weekly minutes via PC, and 47 minutes per week on social networks via tablet devices. J. Clement, "Number of Global Social Network Users 2010–2021," *Statista*, August 14, 2019, https://www.statista.com/statistics/278414/number-of-worldwide-social-network-users/.

[20] Clement, "Number of Internet Users Worldwide."

[21] Richard Hodson, "Special Issue: Digital Revolution," *Nature Outlook*, September 29, 2018, https://www.nature.com/articles/d41586-018-07500-z; Nayan Chanda and Susan Froetschel, *A World Connected: Globalization in the 21st Century* (New Haven, CT: Yale University Press, 2012); Carolyn Lin and David Atkin, eds., *Communication, Technology and Society: New Media Adoption and Uses* (Cresskill, NJ: Hampton Press, 2002); Barry Wellman and Caroline Haythornthwaite, *The Internet in Everyday Life* (Oxford: Blackwell, 2002); Sara Kiesler, ed., *Culture of the Internet* (Mahwah, NJ: Lawrence Erlbaum, 1997).

discussed, cannot keep up with the pace at which microcultures are currently changing and are not capable of reaching the hidden nuances of human behavior that drive them. This was the case for our friend who described her weight loss in the language of "cleanse" rather than "diet." As a result, the practices and norms that consumers engage in and adhere to—the microcultures that they are inadvertently a part of—are being overlooked or downright ignored. While self-reporting may still offer rich information for product design and user experience, it fails during the first part of innovation, when companies are trying to figure out what new opportunity areas they should tap into. It fails because if a consumer is able to articulate and self-report on an opportunity area, it often means that it's too late to innovate in that space—the train has left the proverbial station.

This is a critical point for any business leader who has a team that relies on consumer verbatims to drive innovation.

Ignoring the power of microcultures is thus a costly mistake for businesses, as they end up either overemphasizing opportunities that aren't big enough or undervaluing those opportunities that are ready to make a significant impact on the market.

CHAPTER TWO

Learning from the Masters

In Chapter One, we presented a new way for business professionals to start thinking about innovation. We introduced the concept of microcultures, explaining that these are the nuanced meanings that large numbers of lead consumers assign to a topic and that these meanings indicate the direction that a particular industry, or macroculture, is headed next. We provided real-life examples of the impact microcultures can have on brands, products and overarching categories. And we looked at why it is important to leverage them early in the innovation process, as they can help us uncover more distinct, better defined and more powerful opportunity areas that serve as a foundation for design thinking and consumer cocreating.

In layman's terms, understanding and identifying microcultures helps professionals drastically improve their batting average in innovation projects. But to understand the power of microcultures in the present, we need to understand how they were born from the past. In this chapter, we detail the history of microcultures as a concept and provide their theoretical underpinnings. We show that they are a new interpretation of ideas developed by social scientists starting in the mid-1960s and continuing into the 1980s. By looking at the roots of these ideas, we will more clearly recognize microcultures' capacity as a tool for interpreting shifts in culture and how they will impact the marketplace.

Symbolic Interactionism

Our starting point is the argument that our reality or experience is shaped (and continuously reshaped) by our interactions with others over time. The same goes for our shared assumptions about those realities. This is another way of saying that we don't just react to other people's actions; we *interact* with each other by *interpreting* or *defining* each other's actions. And through this interaction, a certain version of reality is created. What this implies first and foremost is that the world we live in does not have fixed or stable meanings but only our subjective interpretations thereof.[22] What people define as reality can therefore be different in one society versus another or in one particular time period versus another. One only needs to think of the extreme social taboo of marrying across racial lines during the era of segregation in the US (from the late nineteenth century until its abolishment in 1965). Because of the deeply ingrained norms and laws that governed racial identity and, thus, people's understanding and interpretation of skin color, white and black people (categories that are themselves socially constructed) would rarely dare to consider marrying each other—a social fact that seemed perfectly normal to most at the time. By today's standards, such an idea seems ludicrous to the majority of people, with current rates of intermarriage suggesting that what was once considered "abnormal" is now perceived quite differently. According to census data, "one-in-six U.S. newlyweds (17%) were married to a person of a different race or ethnicity in 2015, a more than fivefold increase from 3% in 1967."[23]

---

[22] Peter L. Berger and Thomas Luckmann, *The Social Construction of Reality: A Treatise in the Sociology of Knowledge* (New York: Vintage Books, 1966).

[23] Kirsten Bialik, "Key Facts about Race and Marriage, 50 Years after Loving v. Virginia," *Pew Research Center*, June 12, 2017, https://www.pewresearch.org/fact-tank/2017/06/12/key-facts-about-race-and-marriage-50-years-after-loving-v-virginia/.

19

Perhaps the most important point to take away from this is that *although reality is but a subjective construct, it is rarely perceived as such.* Members of a particular society tend to see the norms, mores and practices that define that society as "natural" or to take them for granted. Let's keep looking at the example of love and marriage to elaborate on this point. In the Western world, we typically associate these two concepts, believing that people who choose to marry do so because they are in love. And our ideas around love are generally driven by images and fantasies (and even mythologies) of a powerful, all-encompassing emotion that is quite inexplicable according to any rational framework. On further investigation however, we will more often than not discover that our marriage choices and the people we fall in love with can quite easily be explained by or reduced to class, income, education and ethnic or racial and religious background. One only needs to glance at current marriage statistics in the US to see, for example, that one's level of education is significant in determining the age at which one decides to get married, whom one ends up marrying (usually someone with the same level of education) and one's chances of staying together in the long run.[24] There are of course exceptions, but by and large, the social institution of marriage is one example of many that *appears* to be determined by one's individual whims and desires but is in reality a product of the societal mechanisms "of interaction that are often rigid to the point of ritual."[25]

This is not to say that people lack free will. Quite the opposite. As mentioned, people actively construct the world they live in through their interpretations and interactions with each other. A famous sociological saying goes, "If men [*sic*] define situations as real, they are real in their consequences."[26] As social beings then, we inevitably

---

[24] Kim Parker and Renee Stepler, "As U.S. Marriage Rate Hovers at 50%, Education Gap in Marital Status Widens," *Pew Research Center*, September 14, 2017, https://www.pewresearch.org/fact-tank/2017/09/14/as-u-s-marriage-rate-hovers-at-50-education-gap-in-marital-status-widens/.

[25] Peter L. Berger, *Invitation to Sociology: A Humanistic Perspective* (New York: Doubleday, 1963), 35.

[26] William I. Thomas and Dorothy S. Thomas, *The Child in America: Behavior Problems and Programs* (New York: Knopf, 1928), 571.

become accustomed to and accept the reality we have collectively constructed. This is quite necessary, because it allows us to maintain internal consistency and get by in the world.

The 1998 film *The Truman Show* offers a biting science-fiction/ fantasy depiction of this theme. Set in a made-up world that is in fact nothing more than the Hollywood set of a reality TV show with one unwitting protagonist (Truman Burbank, played by Jim Carrey), this movie shows us how an individual's particular reality emerges from his interactions with the people around him (in this case, a group of actors whom Truman believes to be his family, friends, neighbors, and so on). Since he has never known anything else, why would he doubt that this is anything but "normal" life? Only when an unusual series of events take place in his early thirties does the protagonist attempt to lift the "veil" off his version of reality. It is with much mental agony that Truman starts to notice what lies in the so-called backstage of his life. Both literally and metaphorically, the film reveals the extent to which *performance* is a fundamental component of the reality we collectively create and subsequently assume as our taken-for-granted world.[27] As sociologist Peter Berger aptly sums up: "One adjusts to a particular society. One matures by becoming habituated to it. One is sane if one shares its cognitive and normative assumptions."[28] That said, it is the work of the social scientist (or the novelist, painter or playwright!) to debunk certain myths, to lay bare the facades of our constructed realities and, ultimately, to better understand the mechanisms that guide and shape human behavior. The concept of microcultures that we are dealing with in this book is a tool for doing just that: dissecting and uncovering those taken-for-granted assumptions and practices that drive and sustain the contemporary world.

When talking about the shared assumptions that emerge from our social interactions and that we use to define reality, we need to also consider how these assumptions and ideas get communicated from person to person and then across entire populations. How does this

---

[27] Erving Goffman, *The Presentation of Self in Everyday Life* (New York: Doubleday, 1959).

[28] Berger, *Invitation to Sociology*, 64.

actually happen? Communication takes place through the *symbolic meanings* that are captured in the words we say (and how we say them), the behaviors we exhibit, the gestures we perform, the clothes we wear, the makeup we (don't) apply, and so on.[29] This particular view of social behavior can be summed up with the following statement: "Humans act toward things on the basis of the meanings they ascribe to those things" and those meanings are, in the first place, created (and continuously re-created) through social interaction.[30] This is yet another way of saying that reality is a subjective construction rather than an objective fact. It emerges from the infinite transactions or forms of communication between people.[31]

It is here that we can situate microcultures, as discussed in Chapter One, and expand on why they can so powerfully explain human behavior in the marketplace. In essence, *microcultures capture the symbolic meanings that individuals create around words, trends, phrases and ideas.* Think about the example of our friend from Chapter One, who explained how she lost 20 lbs by talking about a cleanse rather than a diet. This nuanced distinction present in an individual's (likely subconscious) word choice exactly reflects what we mean by the communication of symbolic meanings. In today's cultural context, the word "cleanse" implies awareness of the dangers that exposure to toxins pose to physical health and the need to care for oneself as a result (e.g., by engaging in a cleanse to rid the body of those toxins). Whereas "diet," on the other hand, has come to signify something else entirely: concern with conventional norms around bodies and thus a submission to patriarchal expectations about what a woman should look like and how she should run her life. The protagonist in our story was simply trying to explain how she lost 20 lbs; she had a number of ways of doing so, and the option she chose tells us a lot about her and

---

[29] Herbert Blumer, *Symbolic Interactionism: Perspective and Method* (Englewood Cliffs, NJ: Prentice-Hall, 1969); Goffmann, *The Presentation of Self in Everyday Life*; George H. Mead, *Mind, Self, and Society: From the Standpoint of a Social Behaviorist* (Chicago: University of Chicago Press, 1934).

[30] Blumer, *Symbolic Interactionism.*

[31] Nicholas Abercombie, Stephen Hill, and Bryan S. Turner, *The Penguin Dictionary of Sociology*, 4th ed. (Harmondsworth: Penguin Publishing, 1984).

other consumers like her. These two seemingly simple words—diet and cleanse—actually carry a tremendous amount of symbolic meaning and explanatory power.

Symbolic interactionism, the theory we are describing here, was first developed in the mid-twentieth century, which means that the kinds of communication it referred to likely took place at work, church, the grocery store, the park or other physical spaces in cities or villages where face-to-face interactions were possible. While that still applies to our current age, the advent of the Internet has meant that much of human communication—and the construction of symbolic meanings that it engenders—has now shifted to the virtual, online realm of social media. The platform might be different but the process is the same: people talking to each other and communicating via meaningful symbols that, in turn, create (and continuously re-create) a particular view of reality.[32]

Let us now consider some cases from our own, online ethnographic research, which we conduct with big data (millions of consumer conversations taking place online over time) and through the lens of microcultures. For example, we started to notice a significant number of online conversations about "premium underwear." We followed up on this term to investigate the specific symbolic meaning it communicated when used online. What we found was that when men talk about buying or wanting to buy "premium underwear," what they are *implicitly communicating* is that they want to find the perfect fit that does not affect the outer appearance of their clothes. They are seeking underwear that fits well under pants without bulking, bagging or riding up and, in particular, underwear that can easily be worn

---

[32] Simon Gottschalk, "The Presentation of Avatars in Second Life: Self and Interaction in Social Virtual Spaces," *Symbolic Interaction* 33, no. 4 (2010): 501–25; Jan Fernback, "Beyond the Diluted Community Concept: A Symbolic Interactionist Perspective on Online Social Relations," *New Media and Society* 9, no. 1 (2007): 49–69; Shanyang Zhao, "The Digital Self: Through the Looking Glass of Telecopresent Others," *Symbolic Interaction* 28, no. 3 (2005): 387–405; Caterina Presi, "Symbolic Interactionism and the Internet: The Communication of Identity in Virtual Communities of Consumption and Real Life" (paper presented at the European Marketing Academy Conference [EMAC], Glasgow, Scotland, May 2003).

under slim-fitting jeans and skinny pants. So, if you are an underwear manufacturer or a retail shop distributing it, it is important to know that by placing a "premium" sticker on your packaging, consumers will be willing to spend more money assuming specific criteria are met.

This is but one example of many. We can equally dissect what consumers really mean when they are talking about buying probiotics and learn that it is driven by a concern for personal longevity and a sense that taking the supplement allows one to take back some control over one's health. We can look at what is driving growth in skin tint products, which turns out to be a desire to project success and ambition through one's appearance. Symbolic capital is gained by showing the world that one does not need a lot of makeup to look good and feel confident. Or we can pull apart the culture of protein bar consumption to uncover that it is a shorthand for helping make the process of weight control easier while simultaneously improving digestion, preventing acid reflux and improving one's sleep. As you will see in the upcoming chapters, each of these types of symbolic meanings generated inadvertently through online consumer interactions offer incredibly rich innovation opportunities for companies big and small. The key then, of course, is the process we employ to identify these symbolic meanings and the context they exist within. But more on this later.

Habitus

Having discussed how we create assumptions about reality and how we communicate those assumptions through interactions and symbolic meanings, let us return to the idea of free will and how this corresponds to the structural forces that underpin society. Structural forces are the broader factors at play in our lives and in the world around us. Examples include anything related to demographics (where we were born, the color of our skin, our ethnic background, our place or year of birth) and how we were brought up and by whom. Structuralist thinkers argue that individuals are more or less at the whim of these forces and are usually unable to change them. As a result, they do not have much control over their behavior or life choices. By the 1960s, this mode of thought largely fell out of favor as it was criticized for being too rigid and out of touch with historical context.[33] (Notably, as mentioned in Chapter One, most consumer research today still relies on such structuralist models for understanding consumer behavior in the marketplace.)

French sociologist Pierre Bourdieu was among a group of (predominantly) French theorists in the 1960s who challenged this deterministic way of thinking and developed a new frame of reference that considers how social structures operate *alongside* human agency (i.e., the decisions that people make in the moment and their reasons for doing so). He coined the term *habitus* to explain that the ways in which people create meaning in a given context are determined by the constant *interactions* between structural forces on the one hand and individual agency on the other. Habitus is another way of describing how we see the world and what compels us to act or react in a particular way; it is especially prevalent in our tastes and practices and can be described as a system of dispositions—how we walk, talk or stand, but also how we feel and think. These dispositions, though, tend to remain invisible to individuals themselves, since they become internalized as second nature and as the normal way of being in the world. That said, as free-thinking individuals, we exercise agency every time we navigate the world; when we express a preference, make a decision or pass a judgment, we are reacting to and interpreting the myriad changes and shifts in meaning taking place around us.

Dispositions then are the lens through which we make sense of this changing world, how we understand the "reality" surrounding us, but also, and perhaps most importantly, *how our consumption choices provide an opportunity to assert our position and gain status or prestige in a particular social world* (what we described in Chapter One as the

---

[33] The significance of historical context became a focus of much discussion and theory in the late 1960s because, to put it simply, it was a time of major social upheavals that ultimately changed the way the world operated. From the wars of decolonization to student uprisings, from the civil rights movement to large-scale protests against the Vietnam War, people's very basic understanding of what they thought they knew about the world was turned on its head.

quest for symbolic capital, which we define in more detail below). For example, the act of bringing an expensive bottle of wine from Italy's celebrated northern Piemonte region to a dinner party allows a person to indicate a number of things: he is a wine connoisseur, which likely implies that he has old European values; he has access to disposable cash; and he has a high regard for the "good things in life." And if, at that same party, someone else were to bring a bottle of craft beer (a newer trend),[34] this might exhibit that person's rejection of industrial production and her tendency to prioritize quality ingredients, innovative recipes, beer flavors and "authenticity." Like the wine connoisseur, the craft beer drinker is probably devoted to the "good things in life" as well but is most likely younger and hipper. All of these meanings are communicated symbolically—that is, not necessarily with spoken words—to the dinner party guests simply through the act of placing these different bottles on the table (we will not digress here by elaborating on the habitus implied by hosting a dinner party to begin with...).

It is also here, in the context of habitus, that Bourdieu elaborates on the concept of *symbolic capital*. We define symbolic capital as a resource that is acquired by exhibiting or drawing on particular forms of knowledge, competencies or skills and interpersonal relationships that, like money, provide access to things. These intangible forms of capital can be converted into other intangible but valuable assets, such as prestige, honor, privilege and acceptance into a particular community and beyond (which, in turn, can also translate into actual capital, that is, money).[35] A university education is perhaps the most

---

[34] "Accounting for 18% of all dollars spent on beer, in 2014 the craft beer sector earned nearly $20 billion in the United States. This equates to a 22% year-on-year dollar sales growth, with exports showing particularly strongly" Drakopoulou Dodd et al., "Habitus Emerging: The Development of Hybrid Logics and Collaborative Business Models in the Irish Craft Beer Sector," *International Small Business Journal: Researching Entrepreneurship* 36, no. 6 (2018): 639–40.

[35] Our definition of symbolic capital is a condensed version of Bourdieu's (1986) lengthier taxonomy of capital into four categories: (1) economic capital (money, property, other tangible assets); (2) cultural capital (forms of knowledge, skills, titles and educational credentials); (3) social capital (who you know; your personal relationships and networks); and, finally, (4) symbolic capital (the

obvious manifestation of this. Irrespective of the fact that you might have spent your university years hungover and skipping class, the mere fact of having somehow attained a university degree—especially if it's from an elite US institution—will open certain doors for you based simply on the value that has been assigned to the degree itself. In other words, the symbolic capital you acquire may have little to do with what you actually learned and more to do with the way "university education" is understood and valued by society at large.

The premise of the 2001 rom-com *Legally Blonde* is a good example of this. Rejected by her longtime boyfriend because he perceives her as not being serious or smart enough (due largely to her blond hair!), the film's protagonist Elle Woods takes on the challenge of being accepted to Harvard Law School as a way of "proving" him wrong. Despite the plot twists in the rest of the movie (that confirm Elle's actual intelligence), this framing of Harvard Law School as synonymous with intelligence and responsibility is what symbolic capital is all about: the meanings that society attaches to certain ideas, practices or beliefs that then become access points to honor, prestige or power.

Microcultures also capture this notion of habitus—the interaction between the structural forces that (partly) determine an individual's behavior and an individual's agency—that is often a means to attaining symbolic capital. For example, if we consider the microcultures around food today, we will find, among others, a growing microculture of concern with the glyphosate herbicide (a commonly known brand name is Monsanto's Roundup); that is, consumers who fear the use of glyphosate in agricultural production.[36] Typically, these consumers

---

outcome of the other forms of capital, that is, the resources available to an individual on the basis of honor, prestige or recognition that come from or are legitimized by the attainment of economic, social or cultural capital).

[36] Part of the increased concern with glyphosate stems from a series of highly publicized lawsuits against the product's manufacturer, German company Bayer (which bought Monsanto in 2018) for failing to adequately warn users of the health risks associated with exposure to glyphosate. Notably, a May 2019 court ruling ordered Bayer to pay $2 billion in damages to a Californian couple who alleged they got cancer from using the herbicide (Tina Bellon, "California Jury Hits Bayer with $2 Billion Award in Roundup Cancer Trial," *Reuters*, May 13, 2019, https://www.reuters.com/article/us-bayer-glyphosate-lawsuit/

are motivated by wanting to display their deeply held beliefs about the corruption of power, the dishonesty of large companies and the truth about environmental destruction. Therefore, consumers who drive this microculture want to be seen as part of a movement that aims to perpetuate the greater good—in this case, the fight against carcinogenic substances. They believe that how and where they spend their money is indicative of their moral standing in society. The symbolic capital they are seeking is to be included among people who stand against corruption and environmental destruction. Thus, they rationalize buying natural or organic alternatives, which they perceive as better for the environment and personal health. In the earlier example we gave of our friend who lost 20 lbs, we can consider her use of the word "cleanse" in similar terms—as a means of attaining symbolic capital such as prestige and acceptance among her peer group of strong female friends.

Of course, these forms of symbolic capital aren't consistent or constant over time. In fact, Bourdieu argues that there is a "tempo" to all of this, in that the symbolic forms of capital keep changing and evolving. At the dinner party noted above, for example, neither the wine nor the beer that the guests drank that night necessarily represented an objective definition of taste; rather, what matters is the social value placed on these products at any given point in time—value or meanings that are always shifting (and competing with each other, which we'll get to below). For example, there's now an emerging concern over the presence of sulfites in traditionally produced wine, which has led to the emergence of organic and biodynamic wines along with new forms of symbolic capital that wine drinkers must now seek in order to gain power or prestige in their circles. This is exactly what microcultures allow us to capture month over month: the nuances of and the changes taking place in the meanings people assign to the world around them and the ideas, trends or topics that inhabit that world.

Let's now take a short detour to Rodeo Drive in LA to look for another example of habitus and its shifting meanings. Because this

---

california-jury-hits-bayer-with-2-billion-award-in-roundup-cancer-trial-idUSKCN1SJ29F).

area is known as the playground of the rich, famous and fashion savvy, we might be surprised to notice a trend of substantially ripped jeans and oversized t-shirts; styles that hardly correspond to the sartorial choices we imagine the rich and famous make. What's going on? A scene from the 2019 Netflix rom-com *Always Be My Maybe* perfectly satirizes this current cultural trend. The film's main character Sasha is a celebrity chef, and in this particular scene she sits with two friends at a chic restaurant waiting for her mystery date to join them (Keanu Reeves playing himself). Marcus, one of the friends, is dressed much more elegantly than everyone else at the restaurant. He doesn't seem to understand why.

"I thought this was a high-end restaurant. Why am I the only one wearing a tux?" Marcus asks sheepishly.

"Oh, sorry, I should have told you," Sasha coolly answers. "Rich people are done with fancy clothes. Now it's all $4000 t-shirts that look as if they were stolen off the homeless."

Inspired in part by punk and grunge cultures, the habitus played out in this scene and on the real-life streets of Rodeo Drive pits structural forces (e.g., someone's class background and income level) against individual agency, that is, the ability of people to go against and challenge what is expected of them given their class position and to make their own fashion choices. In this example, the symbolic capital around clothing has changed as it pertains to wealth or the display of wealth (where prestige now comes from "looking poor").

Field

The habitus—or set of dispositions—that different people display in their everyday lives as they walk, talk, make decisions or show their preferences is also important for another reason: it is responsible for defining the configuration of what Bourdieu calls a *field*: "a structured space of positions within which resources are distributed, usually unequally."[37] A field perhaps most closely resembles a social class (e.g.,

---

[37] Martin J. Packer, *The Science of Qualitative Research* (Cambridge: Cambridge University Press, 2017), 401.

working class, middle class) but is broader in scope, as it can refer to any sort of structured social space. Think of the field of art, the field of politics or the field of education, for example. Each of these fields is guided by its own logic, norms, requirements and habitus, which must be adhered to by those who want to enter into it or by those who want to maintain their position within it (which in turn helps sustain the particular logic, norms, requirements and habitus that define it in the first place). A society is made up of numerous interrelated social fields, and the relationship between them is an arena of struggle: a *battlefield* where individuals and institutions attempt to preserve or overturn the existing distribution of symbolic capital. This is ultimately an endless dispute over the very foundation of identity and hierarchy.[38]

If this sounds familiar, it's because our understanding of microcultures has its roots in this concept of social fields. As explained in Chapter One, the relationship between different microcultures is marked by a struggle for power. Microcultures thus embody interests and conflicts that shape a given reality, as different lead users fight for the power to define that particular microculture. This microculture can eventually begin to define the *macroculture* around a particular idea, industry or trend. Below, an example from our research illustrates what we mean by this *struggle* or *tension* between microcultures. It also shows how these unique conditions in turn create distinctive and nuanced meanings that individuals or groups (subconsciously) communicate according to their own interpretation of what constitutes reality.

In researching the microcultures around plant-based proteins, we discovered two that were particularly significant. On the one hand, we identified a microculture of veganism driving interest in plant-based proteins. This microculture reflects certain apparent meanings: a concern with personal health, animal welfare, environmental pollutants, environmental activism, and so on. Together, these meanings result in a rejection of animal-sourced proteins in favor of plant-based ones because these are perceived as being healthier, harmless to animals, less of an agricultural burden and all around

---

[38] Loïc Wacquant, "Pierre Bourdieu," in *Key Contemporary Thinkers,* 2nd ed., edited by Rob Stone (London and New York: Macmillan, 2008), 269.

more environmentally sustainable. But in the macroculture of plant-based proteins, there's also a competing microculture around the quality of commercially available meat. Here, the meanings that are generated have to do with a consumer's fear of pesticide use in the grains fed to animals, the health risks associated with the prevalent use of carcinogenic pesticides in cattle farming and parents' concerns about what their children eat. And while this microculture—and its associated meanings—around the quality of commercial meat is different from the microculture (and its associated meanings) of veganism, both lead to the same result: increased consumption of plant-based proteins.

We can thus see how microcultures intersect despite ultimately being at odds with each other (while meat eaters tend to ridicule vegans, vegans hold meat eaters in contempt and judge their lack of ethical integrity). The tension between these two microcultures, or *fields*, will at some point result in one dominant microculture that will then have a more significant impact on driving the marketplace of plant-based proteins (of course, there are other microcultures taking part in this struggle as well).

Going back to the Fairlife milk example discussed in Chapter One, we also see a struggle between different microcultures around the broader macroculture of dairy. In recent years, the microculture of health and tolerability dominated and drove the dairy marketplace, as traditional cow's milk plummeted in popularity (in 2018, the sale of traditional cow's milk dropped by more than $1 billion in the US)[39] and ultra-filtered and plant-based milk alternatives took over, satisfying consumers' search for milk that was high in protein, low in sugar and easy to digest. When the Fair Oaks Farm scandal broke with the video released online, consumers were horrified to witness the cruelty that dairy calves and cows were subjected to in the production of Fairlife milk. Because of the speed at which information travels across social media, Fairlife milk was discredited overnight. The microculture of

[39] Carly Sitzer, "US Milk Sales Drop by More Than $1 Billion as Plant-Based Alternatives Take Off," *World Economic Forum*, April 2, 2019, https://www.weforum.org/agenda/2019/04/milk-sales-drop-by-more-than-1-billion-as-plant-based-alternatives-take-off/.

ultra-filtered milk was quickly overtaken by a microculture of plant-based milk alternatives (almond, hemp or oat milk) that communicates, among other things, meanings around animal welfare.

Conclusion

In this chapter, we have gone back to key sociological thinkers from the second half of the twentieth century in order to explain the intellectual roots of microcultures, a concept fundamental to understanding the marketplaces of the twenty-first century. Many business innovators, however, have yet to tap into the power of microcultures; a power that could help them identify the myriad nuances and complexities of consumer behavior. This process is absolutely necessary for successful innovation to take place. For decades, the research industry has relied on a simplistic model to make sense of consumer behavior, which mostly involved taking people's backgrounds and demographic characteristics into account or drawing primarily on self-reported data. In this chapter, we have shown why this has to change. As we have argued, this deterministic model fails to capture all forms of symbolic capital that exist in the numerous intersecting microcultures crowding the marketplace around any given idea, trend or topic and at any given point in time. This outdated model has made the research industry pinpoint specific patterns of behavior that are then typically generalized into segments. As a result, much valuable information is lost or ignored.

As we have explained in detail throughout this chapter, the relationship between structure (i.e., the world "out there") and individual agency (i.e., people choosing to do what they do) is complex. It is guided by unspoken meanings, coded gestures, ever-shifting definitions of reality and struggle—the struggle for power, prestige and "membership" in numerous interrelated social fields of existence or, for our purposes, microcultures. If you don't understand or seek to identify the struggle or tension between microcultures or between lead users, you can't predict the future. Our research model begins here, by accounting for the nuanced meanings and tensions that define not only consumer behavior and its context but the marketplace as a whole and by showing how changes in culture are driving new overall trends over time.

The concept of microcultures pushes us to look *beyond* people's backgrounds and the structural forces that dictate their actions. It teaches us instead that every situation and every human response to that situation is context-dependent. By understanding these fundamental elements of microcultures, we can begin to engage in a more rigorous process of consumer-led research that yields necessary information about the numerous and interrelated opportunity spaces for innovation that are available in the marketplace. In the next chapter, we will outline the three requirements or capabilities of a research methodology (symbolic capital, tension, tempo) that can better equip us for studying microcultures.

Formulating a Microcultures Strategy

CHAPTER THREE

Studying Microcultures: A Methodological Shift

Now that we have introduced the concept of microcultures and shown how they can help us identify new opportunities in the marketplace, the logical next step is to turn our attention to how they can best be studied. In Part Two of this book, we delve into the methodology of microcultures and the strategies required for identifying and decoding them in order to yield value for our innovation and marketing initiatives.

In this chapter, we focus on the requirements for a methodology for the study of microcultures. These are:

1. The identification of symbolic capital in any marketplace context.
2. The ability to pinpoint the various points of tension that constitute a marketplace context.
3. The tempo that moves a marketplace forward—i.e., the speed at which things change within a marketplace context.

Without the fulfillment of these criteria, a research method won't be able to gain a complete understanding of the microcultures that drive a marketplace. In the upcoming pages, we will expand on this by first explaining why traditional methods for trend analysis are not robust enough to detect the symbolic capital, tensions and tempo of microcultures. Consequently, we need a shift in *how* we, as purveyors of insight, think about research and study people, so we can anticipate the cultural movements that are driving growth or threatening the existence of our business. Next, we'll draw on the social-sciences approach of ethnography to explain how the traditional ethnographic method, when adapted for online use with big data, presents perhaps the most rigorous methodology currently available for accessing and decoding the microcultures that make up any marketplace today from a purely consumer-led perspective.[40]

Before moving forward, let's briefly go back to Chapter Two, where we traced the origins of microcultures in the social world and explained how our consumption practices provide an opportunity to assert our position and gain status or prestige in a particular social world. **In other words, we buy things in order to exhibit our symbolic capital, which is an intangible resource such as knowledge, skills or interpersonal relationships that can be translated into prestige, privilege or status.** Symbolic capital lies at the core of all microcultures: it is what drives their formation, what pits them against one another and what

---

[40] There has been a burgeoning of terms and practices in the last two decades to describe the adaptation of the ethnographic method for and of the online realm. For reasons we describe later in this chapter, our preferred term is "big data ethnography." Here is a list of the most common terms that researchers in academia and increasingly industry too are talking about when using online data that employs a particular version or understanding of ethnography in the research process: "'digital ethnography' (Murthy 2008), 'virtual ethnography' (Hine 2000), 'cyberethnography' (Robinson & Schulz 2009), 'discourse-centred online ethnography' (Androutsopoulos 2008), 'internet ethnography' (Boyd 2008; Sade-Beck 2004), 'ethnography on the internet' (Beaulieu 2004), 'ethnography of virtual spaces' (Burrel 2009), 'ethnographic research on the internet' (Garcia et al. 2009), 'internet-related ethnography' (Postill and Pink 2012) and 'netnography' (Kozinets 2009)" (cited in Piia Varis, "Digital Ethnography," *Tilburg Papers in Culture Studies* 104 [August 2014], https://www.tilburguniversity.edu/sites/tiu/files/download/TPCS_104_Varis_2.pdf, 22).

defines their inner workings. Psychologist Ryan Howell explains how the struggle for social prestige (or power) tacitly manifests itself in everyday conversations and interactions: "Many people may say they bought a Mercedes because they appreciate superior precision engineering (a reasonable and socially acceptable explanation), when in reality they bought the car simply because it is a status symbol (not so socially acceptable, so better to confabulate)."[41]

This example is interesting because it shows us, first, how symbolic capital influences consumer choices and behaviors (in this case, why someone is actually buying a Mercedes—because it's a marker of status that makes them look good). Second, it's also a concrete example of how symbolic communication between people and across entire societies occurs in coded or veiled ways (we might say we care about precision engineering, but every time we drive our Mercedes down the street we actually communicate that we have a certain level of wealth and, thus, social status). We might say we're going to Harvard because we respect and want to study with famous "Professor So-and-So," but however true this may be, the meaning that is inadvertently communicated to those around us is that we are highly ambitious, intelligent and probably also relatively wealthy since we can afford Harvard's tuition. These are the intangible resources that people strive to obtain in every decision and interaction. In the consumer context of microcultures, these are the intangible resources that drive purchasing decisions and determine the direction of new demand spaces. After all, why buy just a kumquat when telling someone I buy only organic kumquat rewards me with so much more than the nutrients and calories in the food itself?

Symbolic Capital

If we can understand the forms of symbolic capital that drive a microculture, then we can understand the nuances of meanings that

---

[41] Ryan T. Howell, "Consumer Self-Report Data: You Can Ask What But Not Why," *Psychology Today*, November 17, 2013, https://www.psychologytoday. com/us/blog/cant-buy-happiness/201311/consumer-self-report-data-you-can-ask-what-not-why.

constitute a microculture in the first place. As explained in Chapter Two, the intellectual origins of microcultures can be found in the work of social scientists beginning in the 1960s. As such, in order to detect and make sense of concepts such as symbolic capital and how this shapes microculture, we need a social-sciences-driven methodological approach. What does this mean? First and foremost, it means that we need a form of analysis that can make sense of the unspoken and hidden meanings that guide social relations and human behavior. Because symbolic capital functions in inadvertent and subconscious ways—individuals often cannot readily detect or explain the extent to which their behavior is driven by the struggle for a particular kind of symbolic capital—any method that *directly* asks people for their opinions, interpretations or ideas (e.g., self-reporting, focus groups, surveys) will fail to produce significant or meaningful data. While quantitative analysis is an important aspect of analyzing trends and shifts in the marketplace (more on that later), our primary objective is to find a qualitative methodology based on close *observation* that allows us to detect and interpret the nuances in human behavior.[42]

Ethnographic analysis is the most obvious and powerful methodology for detecting this kind of complexity because it studies groups and people as they go about their regular, everyday lives.[43] Rooted in anthropology, it involves close observation and, ideally, immersion in the day-to-day activities and lives of those being studied.[44]

---

[42] Note: online ethnography blurs the boundaries somewhat between the quantitative/qualitative divide because, although the methodology is primarily observational and thus qualitative in nature, sample sizes are so large that it also enables a quantitative approach. See Annelies Verhaege, Niels Schillewaert, and Emilie van den Berge, "Getting Answers without Asking Questions: The Evaluation of a TV Programme Based on Social Media," *InSites Consulting R&D White Paper Series*, 2009, https://issuu.com/insitesconsulting/docs/04_getting_answers_without_asking_questions.

[43] Robert M. Emerson, Rachel I. Fretz, and Linda L. Shaw, *Writing Ethnographic Fieldnotes* (Chicago: University of Chicago Press, 1995), 2.

[44] Emerson, Fretz, and Shaw, *Writing Ethnographic Fieldnotes*. There is much debate in the social-sciences literature on the merits of covert versus overt field research, specifically in regard to concerns that the researcher who actively becomes part of the research site will inevitably influence and thus bias what

By engaging in this analysis of "natural" behavior, the researcher comes "to enter into the matrix of meanings of the researched, to participate in their system of organized activities, and to feel subject to their code of moral regulation."[45] This is what anthropologist Clifford Geertz calls "thick description": long-term observations that are rich in depth and detail and that can thus provide insight into people's attitudes, beliefs, motivations, values and fears.[46] Erving Goffman's now classic 1961 ethnography, *Asylums: Essays on the Social Situation of Mental Patients and Other Inmates*, shows us how immersion in a research site and close observation of the daily practices of research subjects yields information about the most fundamental aspects of social life and human experience. His ethnography was revolutionary because it was the first to consider the subjective experience of an institution's patients rather than of its doctors or administrators. And in doing so (through near but not complete immersion), he concluded that being a patient in a mental institution had a (mostly negative) influence on one's identity that was similar to that of being an inmate in a prison or a concentration camp, and even similar to that of willing members of a monastery or military organization. In all of these "total institutions"—places where large numbers of similarly situated people are cut off from the outside world and subject to a unique set of formal rules and norms—inmates, patients or members "develop a life of their own that becomes meaningful, reasonable, and normal once you get close to it." A good way to learn about any of these worlds, writes

---

otherwise takes place there. For our purposes, as we will show in a later section, online ethnography allows us to surpass the complexities of overt research and the risks of biasing the research site by eliminating the presence of researchers altogether. For studies that outline the merits of covert ethnographic research, see Howard Schwartz and Jerry Jacobs, *Qualitative Sociology: A Method to the Madness* (New York: The Free Press, 1979); Jack D. Douglas, *Investigative Social Research: Individual and Team Field Research* (Beverly Hills, CA.: Sage Publications, 1976).

[45] Murray L. Wax, "Paradoxes of 'Consent' to the Practice of Fieldwork," *Social Problems* 27 (1980): 272–73.

[46] Clifford Geertz, "Thick Description: Toward an Interpretive Theory of Cultures," in *The Interpretation of Cultures* (New York: Basic Books, 1973), 3–30.

Goffman, is to "submit oneself in the company of the members to the daily round of petty contingencies to which they are subject."[47]

This is not just true for asylums. It enables us to respect, empathize with and understand the consumer condition or the consumer's point of view when searching for the unspoken motivations and needs of the people we are trying to understand. When a major technology company commissioned us to examine the role of personalization in the United States, we were able to go beyond the industry perspective that personalization is merely the act of using technology to identify patterns to better anticipate the behavior of the user. Choosing what type of personalization we allow into our lives is driven by how much and how effectively we want this personalization to impact our self-expression—or, in layman's terms, technology can't just know what I do; I need to believe that it understands the values that make me who I am. If you ask a consumer to try and explain this based on their own view of their experience with their phone or their Alexa, they will think that you are from another planet. They are unaware that the technology in their life can have a profound and emotional impact on how they engage with something made from metal and plastic. But by understanding this deep-rooted emotional need, we can start to uncover opportunities with a deeper understanding of the consumer experience. This understanding is not based on rational or logical journey mapping alone but also on serving the emotional needs of the person asking their phone to play their favorite playlist on Spotify.

Ethnography can teach us a lot about the intricacies of human behavior and everyday life, the construction of identity and the beliefs, values and worldviews underlying human action and social life[48]—exactly those characteristics that we need in order to understand how the inadvertent meanings around symbolic capital are created and how they manifest in microculture.

---

[47] Erving Goffman, *Asylums: Essays on the Social Situation of Mental Patients and Other Inmates* (New York: Anchor Books, 1961), x.

[48] Angela C. Garcia et al., "Ethnographic Approaches to the Internet and Computer-Mediated Communication," *Journal of Contemporary Ethnography* 38, no. 1 (2009): 53.

Tension

Next, a methodology should have the capability to detect *tension* within and between microcultures. This tension refers to the power struggle that inevitably exists *between* but also *within* microcultures. As mentioned, microcultures consist of multiple and ever-changing forms of symbolic capital, each of which is in a constant state of tension with the other forms as they struggle to secure power and status. This includes fighting to define identity or to make one idea or meaning dominant over another.

Let's take the feminist movement, with its numerous internal divisions, as an example. While you might be able to place everyone who is fighting for equal rights for women under the banner of "feminism," on closer inspection it is obvious that this ideological field or arena is extremely divided and made up of numerous subgroups, each with its own agenda, goals and objectives. To simplify the issue, we might say that in the US (as in other parts of the world), the most central division within the feminist movement is between the second wave and the third wave of feminists. The former, also called mainstream feminism, developed in the 1960s. This group of feminists was fighting against the patriarchy, specifically against the discrimination of women in educational institutions and the workplace. They banded together to try and establish legislation against this discrimination and promote the entry and acceptance of women into educational and professional spaces. While they succeeded in many ways—women nowadays go to college and are part of the workforce at pretty much the same rate as men (although they still deal with lower salaries, fewer opportunities for professional advancement and more workplace harassment)—this movement was led almost exclusively by white, middle-class women, which meant that mostly their own, unique interests were represented in the struggle. It was not until the mid-1990s, when a new generation came of age, that the principles of the feminist movement were redefined and expanded to include the specific experiences of women of color, economically disadvantaged women, women of the Global South, lesbian women, and so on.

This new movement of third-wave feminists had unique objectives and guiding principles (e.g., challenging essentialist definitions of womanhood), and the *meanings* that defined its struggle were different from those of the second-wave feminists. For example, third-wave feminists focused on creating overlap with the environmental movement, since they argue that women of color and/or poor women are the most vulnerable in the face of environmental degradation and catastrophe. A perfect example of this is the fact that black women were disproportionately affected by the devastation brought on by Hurricane Katrina in 2005. Third-wave feminists highlight that this happened because this group was already one of the poorest in the US at the time and thus had less resources to deal with the disaster and its aftermath. This was not a new problem; it was something that could be traced back to the history of slavery in Louisiana.[49]

So, despite the fact that both second- and third-wave feminists ultimately share the goal of fighting for women's equal rights, tension exists. And this tension is complex, nuanced and overlapping. To the untrained eye, the groups may seem to share a purpose, but closer examination reveals that in many instances, their cultures are actually in opposition to each other. Traditional survey-based methodologies would be hard-pressed to adequately reveal these nuances or uncover these warring beliefs. This is because survey-based methods rely on what people themselves are capable of identifying and then articulating. As we've highlighted in previous chapters, microcultures happen inadvertently. People are not necessarily aware that they are embedded in them or do not have the ability to clearly articulate their beliefs or motivations. Going back to our feminism example, while we can assume that people who are part of this movement are aware of their embeddedness in it or of why they are fighting for its goals, self-reporting would still fall short of explaining the entire story. Detecting the nuanced meanings that govern the organization of a particular group and the tensions that inevitably emerge and

---

[49] Spike Lee (dir.), *When the Levees Broke: A Requiem in Four Acts*, HBO, 2006; see also Barbara Ransby, "Katrina, Black Women, and the Deadly Discourse on Black Poverty in America," *Du Bois Review: Social Science Research on Race* 3, no. 1 (2006): 215–22.

define its dynamic would take a skilled ethnographer who is capable of immersing herself in her research field—say, in a community of transgender environmental activists in California or in a group of white women in North Carolina rallying to prevent federal defunding of Planned Parenthood—who can establish trust among her research subjects and who has the luxury of extended time (months, if not years) to carefully observe this particular context.

Or, let's briefly consider another example: Jesus and homosexuality. You may have various organized groups of people who believe in Jesus, but there are obvious differences and thus tensions between a Catholic and a Protestant interpretation of Jesus and even a Jewish understanding of the historical Jesus. The different meanings attributed to Jesus by these different religions will result in very different practices and beliefs. The Unitarian Church, for example, accepts and welcomes gay people into its congregation while also believing that Jesus, although he was inspired by God and his moral teachings, is not himself a savior or a deity, a fact that can be explained by Unitarians' use of modern science rather than religious dogma. In the Catholic Church on the other hand, which is guided by the principle of original sin and Jesus as the embodiment of salvation, homosexuality remains controversial and divisive.

Again, it would require a skilled ethnographer to immerse himself into these various religious communities in order to identify and make sense of these various belief systems and the conflicts that emerge as a result. However, although trained social scientists who engage in immersive ethnographic analysis *can* in fact account for the tensions and inadvertent meanings of social life (as Goffman did in his groundbreaking *Asylums* study), there are limitations when applying the traditional ethnographic method to the consumer marketplace. Most significantly, traditional ethnography is a slow, timely and often expensive methodology that can really treat only small samples adequately, generally during one moment in time (sometimes, of course, a researcher can return to the field for additional observations, but this requires more time and more money). Moreover, the limitations of a small sample would make it impossible to know, for example, if the symbolic capital and tensions identified are all-encompassing trends or just reflective of a small group or portion of the market.

Tempo

This brings us to the third and last key characteristic that a methodology must be capable of detecting in order to meaningfully study microcultures: tempo.

In our modern world of digital connectedness, information travels at breakneck speeds and people communicate with each other like never before in human history. As a result, the tempo of microcultures (of the nuances and meanings that people assign to the world around them) is highly variable. When transposed into the marketplace, this means that consumer trends are in a constant state of flux. One only has to think of the dramatic fluctuations in the "green" household cleaning industry, which was virtually unknown about a decade ago but then exploded on the market as sales of eco-friendly, natural and organic cleaning alternatives more than doubled from $303 million in 2007 to $640 million in 2011.[50] This boom, however, was suddenly followed by a period of stagnation and even decline.[51] In recent years, there has been another upward trend in green household cleaning products, primarily with mass-marketed brands such as Clorox Green Works or private label brands from giants such as Walmart, which introduced an all-natural line of affordable cleaning products in 2013 with huge success.[52] Now, the global market for natural and plant-based household cleaners is projected to grow from $17.90 billion in 2017 to $27.83 billion by 2024.[53]

---

[50] Packaged Fact, "Green Cleaning Products in the U.S.," August 31, 2012, https://www.packagedfacts.com/Green-Cleaning-Products-7114196/.

[51] Packaged Fact, "Green Household Cleaning and Laundry Products in the U.S., 3rd Edition," March 13, 2015, https://www.packagedfacts.com/Green-Household-Cleaning-8825323/.

[52] Packaged Fact, "Green Household Cleaning."

[53] MarketWatch, "Household Green Cleaning Products Market Worth $27.83 Billion by 2024 – Exclusive Report by 360iResearch," *MarketWatch*, April 24, 2019, https://www.marketwatch.com/press-release/household-green-cleaning

What dominates the market today is thus no guarantee of popularity tomorrow. In the past, cataclysmic events such as war or epidemics influenced broad-sweeping changes across society. Today, everything simply moves faster, and because information is so easy to come by, meanings and opinions change at lightning speed. As we saw with the Fairlife milk example, the release of a scathing video across social media transformed the reputation and cachet of a product *overnight*. Before the video was released, the meanings around Fairlife milk were positive: the product contributed to health and tolerability of dairy. The day after the video was released, the new meaning generated around Fairlife milk—animal cruelty—was suddenly detrimental to the product's future and a threat to its leadership position in the marketplace. In turn, the symbolic capital in the macroculture of dairy shifted as well: when buying dairy (or a dairy alternative), consumers were now more concerned about displaying their concern for the welfare of animals rather than concern for their personal health and tolerability of the product.

Because microcultures change and evolve from month to month, it is necessary to capture the nuances of these changes in order to understand where we're headed so that we can better predict the future. Thus, we need to constantly ask ourselves: "What happens to a trend once it is born?" and "How will it survive consumer culture?"

To answer such questions, a methodological tool is required that can measure both the tempo of the marketplace as well as identify the microcultures behind it. Traditional ethnographic methods are extremely valuable for gaining deep insight into the norms, rituals and meanings of any given social world (making them powerful tools for examining symbolic capital and the tensions around and between microcultures) but are not robust enough for analyzing the nonstop creation of new meanings in our hyperconnected and digitized modern-day lives. Further, because ethnography requires

47

such in-depth observation and analysis, it is a rather slow research method that mostly captures only one moment in time. In today's fast-paced business world, the kind of in-depth observation and immersion needed to understand the variable nature of the marketplace would have to take place monthly. No one, neither big nor small companies, has the resources for this.

Before introducing the solution to this problem—adapting the ethnographic method for online use with big data—let's look at an example, namely the evolution of the Occupy movement. This will provide us with a clearer sense of why it is so important to understand the context and scope of microcultures, especially as they evolve and change over time.

Imagine you are a reporter walking around Manhattan's financial district on September 17, 2011—the day the Occupy movement is said to have started—trying to make sense of what is going on. You have been sent out to cover a protest march of about one thousand people that is making its way down Wall Street. A couple of hours later, the protest winds its way to Zuccotti Park in lower Manhattan. You notice a fairly large group of punk-like kids setting up tents in one area of the park while, in another, they are playing drums and rolling joints.

In these early days of the "movement," it seems to consist of a confused group of anarchists or hippies looking to get into trouble. This can't be more than an isolated and fringe configuration of protestors, you think, looking around at the crowd that has gathered: a sea of angry young faces and an abundance of vintage t-shirts with slogans from the 1960s ("Food, Not Bombs," "Viva Zapatista, No NAFTA"). But two days later, you return to Zuccotti Park and notice that it's looking considerably more organized and *permanent*, with tents set up in one corner, meeting areas in another, a food supply chain in place with enough donated food for three thousand meals a day, a library, and even a newspaper and around-the-clock volunteer medical staff offering free healthcare.[54] A large collection of protest placards lean against the park's fencing, displaying slogans that all seem to coalesce

---

[54] Jeff Sharlet, "Inside Occupy Wall Street," *Rolling Stone*, November 11, 2011, https://www.rollingstone.com/politics/politics-news/inside-occupy-wall-street-236993/.

around a similar theme: "Wall Street Is Destroying America," "People Not Profits," "Smash Wall Street" and "We Are the 99%." You find out from survey data that yes, 64% of those in the movement are under the age of 35, but one-third of participants are older than 35, and one-fifth are 45 or older; and about half of the movement's participants are employed full-time[55]—this is certainly not a movement of fringe anarchists or hippies, you realize. There are all kinds of people here: "cooks and nannies and librarians, lots of librarians, and Teamsters and priests and immigrants, legal and otherwise, and culture jammers, eco-warriors, hackers, and men and women in Guy Fawkes masks, an army of stunt doubles from V for Vendetta, all joined by young veterans of the Arab Spring and the revolts in Greece and Spain."[56]

In less than a month, the protest has spread to more US cities; thousands of people are now marching across Boston, Washington DC, Chicago, and LA. By October 15, less than a month since the initial protest on Wall Street, demonstrations inspired by Occupy are taking place in 951 cities across 82 countries worldwide.[57]

As we know now, in retrospect, Occupy was anything but a fringe movement of unruly "punk" kids. While its achievements are debatable, it unquestionably became a major movement across the US and beyond, and it influenced subsequent activist movements such as Black Lives Matter. In retrospect, we also know that the movement originally gathered inspiration and momentum from other major public protests that preceded it, such as the Arab Spring—which originated in Cairo's Tahrir Square in January 2011—and the "Real Democracy Now" movement against European austerity that began in Madrid's Puerta del Sol Square, in May of the same year.

The Occupy movement is an interesting example because it shows us that we need a "wide angle lens" in order to interpret and make

---

[55] Sean Captain, "The Demographics of Occupy Wall Street," *Fast Company*, October 19, 2011, https://www.fastcompany.com/1789018/demographics-occupy-wall-street.

[56] Sharlet, "Inside Occupy Wall Street."

[57] Bill Chappell, "Occupy Wall Street: From A Blog Post To A Movement," *National Public Radio (NPR)*, October 20, 2011, https://www.npr.org/2011/10/20/141530025/occupy-wall-street-from-a-blog-post-to-a-movement.

sense of how microcultures take form and change over time. The movement is also significant because it is emblematic of our times: it started with an online blog post and eventually spread like wildfire across the country before gaining momentum across the world. A couple of months before the first protest march, the "movement" was already well underway with its own website, Twitter account and Facebook page, all of which were being used to promote the first rally on Wall Street on September 17, 2011, and instructed protestors to "bring tents."[58] Things evolved at record speed as more groups joined, original goals broke down while new ones took shape, all while police surveillance and occasional violent raids threatened to shut down the operation. This finally happened during a surprise raid on the night of November 15, 2011, when police tore down tents and arrested about seventy people as they cleared out the Occupy encampment in Zuccotti Park.[59] And thus ended a fifty-nine-day social and political movement, whose objectives fluctuated constantly during that short period and whose impact is still being disputed today, eight years later. In short, the Occupy movement reminds us how much insight into the context and significance of an event we lose if we don't have a temporal scope that allows us to measure change *as an event is happening* and in its aftermath.

It is here that we turn our attention to online ethnography, also known as virtual ethnography, cyber ethnography, netnography or social media netnography. Based on the principles of immersive observational ethnography discussed above, the online adaptation moves away from the traditional face-to-face model and focuses instead on close observation of everyday human activities as they take place online.[60] The ability to capture people's "natural" everyday

---

58 Sharlet, "Inside Occupy Wall Street"; Jana Kasperkevic, "Occupy Wall Street: Four Years Later," *Guardian*, September 16, 2015, https://www.theguardian.com/world/ng-interactive/2015/sep/16/occupy-wall-street-four-years-later-timeline.

59 Joe Weisenthal and Robert Johnson, "Here's How Occupy Wall Street Came to a Sudden, Unexpected End Today," *Business Insider*, November 15, 2011, https://www.businessinsider.com/how-police-cleared-occupy-wall-street-2011-11.

60 Garcia et al., "Ethnographic Approaches to the Internet"; Verhaege, Schillewaert, and van den Berge, "Getting Answers without Asking Questions"; Christine Hine, *Virtual Ethnography* (London: Sage, 2000).

behavior remains at the center of this modified methodology. A major difference between traditional and online ethnography is that the latter does not *directly* observe the research subject; thus, the "interaction" between researcher and subject remains mostly anonymous and/or noninvasive. There are several important implications of this, including a significant reduction—if not complete elimination—of interview bias (research subjects are just "being," communicating online in natural and non-prompted ways rather than responding to and possibly altering their behavior in the presence of an interviewer/researcher). The anonymity of online ethnography also reduces instances of respondents lying in order to save face when it comes to sensitive topics. Taboo loses its power when you are protected by a pseudonym.

Let's take menstruation as an example. We were commissioned by a Fortune 1000 company to help them understand the culture of managing menstrual pain. It is generally difficult to obtain rich, in-depth data on this topic because it is historically sensitive and culturally "taboo." But online ethnography allowed us to be a fly on the wall, as large samples of women engaged online. We could overcome the traditional alibis that women would share in a focus group and eliminate the bias of the research to get to a deeper, rawer representation of women's experience of living with and managing menstrual pain.

What we found was that a significant portion of the core market around menstrual pain (it's worth noting that this is a substantially sized market of more than ninety million consumers in the US) was concerned with pain acknowledgment: many women talked about the frustration of having their menstrual pains dismissed or minimized and tried to find ways of having their pain recognized. This concern manifested in frequent online conversations about kidney pain, which we then interpreted as a strategy that women employ to render their menstrual symptoms more universal (i.e., less woman-focused) in the hope of being taken more seriously. For our client, this was valuable information for product development and marketing, as they could now confidently engage in a business plan that legitimizes the pain experienced by its consumer base by communicating that "your pain is real" and that menstrual pain could possibly affect other areas of health.

A key element of the kind of online ethnography we are describing here is big data. Defined as "extremely large data sets that may be analyzed computationally to reveal patterns, trends, and associations, especially relating to human behavior and interactions,"[61] big data used in conjunction with the ethnographic method enables researchers to observe and interpret the *billions* of interactions taking place online, in detail, in depth and at any given point in time. Researcher Tricia Wang calls this "thick data": the nuanced meanings—stories, compelling arguments, insightful details—that lie behind big data visualization and analysis.[62] "Big Data," she writes, "reveals insights with a particular range of data points, while Thick Data [which is derived from ethnographic analysis] reveals the social context of and connections between data points."[63]

The intersection or mixed methodology of big data analysis and ethnography provides us with the social context and nuanced meanings that exist within microcultures while also capturing the temporal scope or rate of change of these contexts and meanings over time. When applied to significantly sized samples, this mixed method enables the quantification of ethnographic insight.[64] In turn, this allows us to identify the hidden meanings that consumers

---

[61] https://www.cbronline.com/what-is/what-is-big-data-4899770/.

[62] This concept is based on Clifford Geertz's call for "thick description" in ethnographic research: amassing observations from the field that are rich in depth and detail so as to more profoundly make sense of human behavior and social interaction (see the first part of this chapter). Cited from Tricia Wang, "Big Data Needs Thick Data," *Ethnography Matters*, May 13, 2013, http://ethnographymatters.net/blog/2013/05/13/big-data-needs-thick-data/.

[63] Wang, "Big Data Needs Thick Data."

[64] Vincent Charles and Tatiana Gherman, "Big Data Analytics and Ethnography: Together for the Greater Good," in *Big Data for the Greater Good: Studies in Big Data* vol. 42, Ali Emrouznejad and Charles Vincent, eds. (Cham, Switzerland: Springer, 2018), 19–33; Joonas Rokka and Lionel Sitz, "Why Teach Ethnography to Managers (in the Big Data Era)?" *The Conversation*, October 10, 2018, https://theconversation.com/why-teach-ethnography-to-managers-in-the-big-data-era-104669.

inadvertently create in each of their online interactions (as people do offline as well).

When we talk about *big data ethnography*, what we mean concretely is that we rely on the computational power of algorithms (i.e., machine learning) to identify meanings and then capture and "measure" the relative strength of each meaning that consumers associate with a particular topic over time (i.e., the search term under consideration). Context is key here, that is, the cultural context in which a particular topic or trend is placed. Without this context, you won't be able to do much more than engage in basic pattern recognition.

But what exactly do we mean by context? First and foremost, to truly understand the cultural context in which consumers express ideas, beliefs and values, we need immersive methods that are able to *go beyond direct mentions of a particular topic* in order to understand *the universe of topics or meanings surrounding a search term*: the interrelated or overlapping topics that consumers discuss in the context of the original search term. In other words, we can't just focus on the online conversations that directly mention our search term or topic of interest but we also need a mechanism or tool for analyzing the impact of topics *indirectly* connected through other topics to our topic of interest.

Let's back up for a moment. As we explained, ethnography is about understanding meanings. Online, consumers inadvertently communicate meanings around any and all topics through their interactions on platforms that enable long-form communication with some amount of anonymity (forums, comments under blogs, YouTube videos, product reviews, etc.). While anyone can scrape these publicly accessible conversations, one major problem remains: in order to do what an ethnographer would do, it is necessary to understand and distinguish between *contexts.*

This is now possible with modern technologies like artificial intelligence (AI) and machine learning. We can teach a machine to understand context online the same way a human ethnographer can offline while observing a conversation at a dinner party, for example.

Imagine the kind of dinner party conversation first: four people are sitting at a table and get onto the topic of probiotics for about fifteen minutes. At first, the conversation flows, as everyone is referring in some way to the topic of probiotics, even if they're not always actually saying or repeating the word itself. Someone at the table talks about her gut health. Then someone else mentions an interest in increasing the amount of fermented foods he has in his diet. Then another person talks about taking supplements to boost her immunity. All of these comments make it clear to an ethnographer that these three people are responding on-topic, adding to what we know probiotics mean to consumers (meanings around gut health, digestion, diet or immunity). But then, about halfway through the conversation, a fourth person at the table goes off on a tangent to talk about something his kids did because he received a text from his partner. This is out of context and irrelevant. The ethnographer knows to ignore this.

In the online variant of this conversation, where there can be thousands of responses to a particular post on a specific topic like probiotics, machines are trained to identify in-context and out-of-context responses. Like in the dinner table conversation, a machine would know which responses from other users in the same thread— and elsewhere online—are related to and part of the same context of probiotics. And, like in the dinner table conversation, the machine would also know to ignore the out-of-context comments.

Taking the in-context responses, the machine has to identify the major topics within them. As an example, let's consider what our conversation about probiotics at the dinner table would look like if it took place on an online forum. Imagine that someone starts a new thread by talking about probiotic supplements, asking what people think of a particular brand. Within seconds, someone reacts to this first post by talking about his own gut health and that he's looking for foods that might help improve his poor digestion. He never actually uses the word "probiotic" but it's clear, when looking at the context of the conversation thread, that he is responding directly to the first poster talking about probiotic supplements. Then a third person adds a message, this time about the high cost of probiotic supplements, which he finds frustrating and which makes him less eager to make probiotics a regular part of his nutritional regimen. And then a fourth person joins the thread. She talks about feeling more in control of her health by boosting her immunity through kombucha, which she has recently learned how to make herself (again, this poster never actually mentions the word probiotic, but the "AI ethnographer," that is, the machine, is able to recognize that she's talking about it based on the context of the thread). All in all, these are nothing but the meanings associated with probiotics. For example, comments about "digestion," "immunity," and so on provide additional meaning to the microculture of probiotics.

Much like the (human) ethnographer at the dinner party, the AI ethnographer recognizes that all three of these posters have created new meanings around the topic of probiotics in their responses to the original poster's question about a particular brand of probiotic supplements. Traditional ethnography would be well equipped to dig into the nuances of this kind of conversation and make sense of the more minute and underlying meanings being exchanged across the dinner party version of this conversation. But when these conversations take place online, it is not simply four people chatting around a candle-lit table but hundreds of thousands communicating across multiple online platforms. Unlike the dinner party conversation, where a limited number of ideas will be generated in the course of fifteen minutes, online conversations generate tens if not hundreds of thousands of data points in the same amount of time. Notably, the machine weeds out and eliminates irrelevant posts—the trolling comments, the divergences, and so on— from the equation in the same way that the ethnographer at the dinner table ignores the tangent about one of the guest's kids.

What's more, the AI ethnographer is capable of not only detecting the broader context around search terms but also computing the nature of the relationships between them (e.g., volume, frequency, semantic distance). It can turn the frequency and volume with which consumers associate contextual topics with probiotics into a mathematical number—a distance calculation if you will, something that informs us about each related topic's contextual importance to the conversation or topic as a whole. In other words, the machine takes all the (relevant) responses into account, converts them into topics— calculating the semantic distance between the various topics and the searched-for topic of "probiotics"—and then reports this temporally.

Another example: in one of the online ethnographies we conducted, we found that in 2017, the context of conversations around probiotics—what we referred to above as the *universe of meanings* or *cultural universe* in an algorithmic mapping of a topic or trend—was all about supplements. In other words, the topics that we detected lying in close proximity to probiotics were linked to supplementation. A year later, in 2018, when we searching for the same term, "probiotic," we noticed a slight change: a new set of meanings had been created in the context of probiotics. Supplements were still significant but were semantically more distant from the core discussion of probiotics. In its place, a focus on changes in eating habits had developed. Large numbers of people were now talking about introducing fermented foods and drinks into their diet, such as sauerkraut, kombucha or kefir.

How did we know this? As mentioned, big data ethnography provides its researchers with the context; the entire "cultural universe" that exists around a particular topic or trend and that is generated either directly or indirectly through the numerous conversations happening online. Typical analytics platforms, by contrast, will ignore all responses or comments that don't *directly* use the original search term (probiotic in this case). This means missing out on the opportunity to truly enable an ethnographic analysis. Using AI technology, big data ethnography analyzes millions of consumer review sites, forum threads and other online social media conversations about millions of products across hundreds of categories. It looks both for conversations in direct connection to the topic of concern and for all of the other topics that people mention across the web—without necessarily using the term itself—within the context of the original search term. In this way, you're able to determine and calculate which of these topics is *more* or *less* relevant to the microculture of probiotics.

Think about the implication of this in the context of protecting your brands, products and investments.

Let's imagine that you are McDonald's. With traditional big data tools and rudimentary social media listening platforms, the machine is looking to identify, gather and analyze when consumers have talked about or said "McDonald's" and linked it with another topic or word. This will tell you that more consumers are calling McDonald's "fast food" this month versus last month, or that more people are talking about the "Big Mac" than about the "Filet-o-Fish." While this is something of an oversimplification, and there is in fact insight to be gained by linking this type of information to other data inputs (say sales or purchase data in order to identify behavioral patterns), this lacks deeper, more contextualized cultural significance.

Instead, imagine that we not only look for instances where consumers are referencing "McDonald's" and recognize that a large portion of the population is associating McDonald's with "fast food," but that we also see that in the absence of the term McDonald's, "fast food" is increasingly being associated with the notion of "empty calories." In fact, we notice that this connection between "fast food" and "empty calories" is so strong that it is now also impacting the meanings that people associate with McDonald's itself. That is, through indirect association, McDonald's is now becoming about empty calories. This chain of meaning can be understood only if we study the full context of conversations around McDonald's and not just the specific mentions of the topic. Doing so not only enables true ethnographic observation but also transforms our understanding of trends, ideas and even brands and companies. Understanding the context allows us to understand how a relatively small cultural meaning can shape other small cultural meanings to eventually determine how we understand, interpret and talk about a particular topic or set of topics.

Machine learning enables this kind of context mapping and thus allows us to very quickly conduct in-depth observational ethnographic analysis with big data (millions of consumer conversations happening over time, online). This in turn ensures that we understand what's really going on in a particular microculture and how that microculture (and the forms of symbolic capital it represents) might be changing. It enables us to understand which meanings are more or less important in the context under analysis, which are new and emerging or old and dying, and which change the most month by month. Most importantly, this mixed method of big data-based ethnography helps us identify how certain meanings cluster to create microcultures within a broader macroculture. It also allows us to quantify the existing marketplace (how many people are interested in a macro- or microculture) and the rate of change, which eventually leads to new capabilities in prediction and forecasting as well.

Let's return to the probiotics example. Big data ethnography reveals that supplementation has moved "further away" in semantic distance from the core of probiotics. That distance *away from* or *inward toward* a particular topic is what allows us to understand changes in the meanings that circulate around a particular topic. A machine is then able to use that understanding to run a whole series of calculations to help us understand *how fast* something might be changing. Having this kind of analysis enables us as researchers and innovation professionals to take this seemingly slight semantic shift in how people talk about a topic like probiotics—in this case, from probiotic supplements to fermented food and drink—to calculate the impact of that change in terms of the overall market potential for probiotics, its growth rate and level of maturity in adoption.

Because we work with big data in this mixed method, we have the capacity to analyze hundreds of thousands of data points connected to probiotics—leveraged from the kinds of online conversations described above—to not only understand all the meanings being generated in these discussions but also understand *which* meanings are more important to consumers at any given point in time. This means that we are able to assign actual values to consumer-generated meanings and see patterns that we'd otherwise miss—leading to the identification of microcultures around fermentation and fermented foods, for example.

The real power of big data ethnography is exactly this marriage of its two parts: the *quantitative* significance of large sample sizes (big data) and the *qualitative* value of detailed and in-depth observation (ethnography), albeit aided by a machine.

Big data ethnography is ultimately about taking complex ideas from the social sciences—as discussed in Chapter Two: the human perception of reality, how people construct meaning, the coded ways in which communication takes place, the social struggle for power and status, the constant flux of what constitutes status—and translating them into mathematical ideas that then become measurable quantitatively *and* qualitatively. This allows us to transform research for the purpose of innovation by analyzing the hundreds of thousands of nuanced meanings that people generate around microcultures and to measure the changes in the configuration of those microcultures. Big data ethnography also provides access to temporal data that is charted from one month to another or from one quarter to another—a process that would be impossible for the lone human ethnographer to engage in due to real-life parameters and limitations, including time and money.

Conclusion

As we have shown in this chapter, social sciences-driven methodologies are a starting point for examining and making sense of the nuanced landscape of consumer-created microcultures. Traditional ethnographic models have the power to detect the complex meanings and tensions of consumer behavior but lack the ability to measure the tempo of our hyperconnected and ever-changing world. Data input thus needs to be big, temporal and agile. This is the only way in which we, as innovation specialists, can transform the first part of the innovation process. Big data arms us with a complete picture of a particular trend, idea or social phenomenon. It includes all the forms of meanings generated in culture, the tempo at which culture moves, and the tensions within and between different microcultures. Perhaps most importantly, big data helps us determine which meanings are winning and which ones are on their way out.

Now that we have outlined the methodology required to study microcultures, the next chapter will go deeper to help you recognize and decode the five patterns that microcultures most commonly exhibit so that you can begin to put the theory into practice.

CHAPTER FOUR

The Five Patterns Exhibited by Microcultures

Now that we know why microcultures exist and how you can study them, it is time to learn about some of the different characteristics they exhibit. So, in this chapter we will continue to talk about microcultures from the consumer's perspective, but we will also outline in detail the five main characteristics that microcultures exhibit with the purpose of helping you identify them easily during the research process.

It is important to note that while some microcultures may exhibit all five of the characteristics discussed here simultaneously, this is rarely the case. Typically, only one or two characteristics will be present. And often, one characteristic drives the creation of the next. However, for the sake of simplicity, let's look at each pattern individually and find a corresponding example. With this knowledge and understanding in hand, you will be able to more readily identify and decode a microculture so that you can then leverage its power to identify and quantify new revenue opportunities for your business.

Microculture Characteristic #1: The Introduction of a Net New Idea

The first characteristic that a microculture may exhibit is that it introduces *an altogether new idea to the marketplace.* This is where a new concept is born and takes hold in the marketplace. It begins as a small movement or niche solution but it can, in time, grow to the point that it crosses over into the mainstream. It can cannibalize other solutions in its category or force other solutions to drastically change because it transforms norms, rituals and established meanings in culture. One example is coworking spaces.

The microculture of coworking spaces didn't exist less than fifteen years ago. As Brad Neuberg (the man who coined the term *coworking* in San Francisco in 2005) said, "there were other proto-ideas that had a coworking like aspect before such as artist colonies, journalist newsrooms, and rent-a-office spaces … (but) none of them had the *open community* aspect of coworking."[65]

Today, there are close to nineteen thousand coworking spaces worldwide—a figure that has more than doubled in the last five years.[66] Situated in the broader macroculture of work, the microculture of coworking has gained mainstream status and is having a major influence on the design and operation of traditional office spaces at some of the world's largest corporations.

So what happened here? Was Brad a multi-millionaire genius who identified a gap in the market, and thus set out to disrupt the real estate and office design industry? Was this a calculated corporate ploy, born from foundational research, swot analysis and massive investment in development, marketing and infrastructure? Quite the contrary. It began with Brad borrowing $300 from his father. He then rented a small space on Mondays and Tuesdays at the Spiral Muse feminist collective in San Francisco's Mission district. Neuberg would

---

[65] Brad Neuberg, "The Start of Coworking (from the Guy That Started It)," *Coding in Paradise* (blog), no date, accessed July 22, 2019: http://codinginparadise.org/ebooks/html/blog/start_of_coworking.html. Emphasis added.

[66] E. Mazareanu, "Number of Coworking Spaces in the United States from 2007 to 2022," *Statista*, August 9, 2019, https://www.statista.com/statistics/797546/number-of-coworking-spaces-us/.

go to Spiral Muse every Monday and Tuesday and set up folding card tables in anticipation of others who might join him.

He waited. And no one came.

Then, he started dropping off flyers at local coffee shops. He interrupted people on their computers at restaurants. He waited for people to finish calls in their car to ask them if they needed a place to work. Finally, a small trickle of curious onlookers started passing by to see what he was talking about. Then one person, a start-up developer, became Neuberg's first official paying "coworker." The Spiral Muse coworking space ran for about a year and, once he closed it down, Neuberg started a new coworking space with ten volunteers at a large work/live loft called the Hat Factory.[67]

Today, coworking spaces have blossomed into a global phenomenon, with start-ups like WeWork and IWG/Regus dominating the field (WeWork was valued at $47 billion as of June 2019 and was the world's fastest growing coworking company in 2017).[68] Coworking spaces typically serve freelancers, "laptop nomads," remote workers, small to medium enterprises and start-ups or early stage ventures who have uncertain business growth rates and are not quite ready to invest in long-term leases. As the number of one-person or nonemployer businesses continues to grow in the US (with a 2% increase from 24.3 million in 2015 to 24.8 million in 2016, according to the US Census Bureau[69]) and technological advances make where and how you work more flexible (thanks to the use of laptops and smartphones), the need for communal work environments has grown too.[70]

But coworking spaces are not just about renting a desk or an

---

[67] Neuberg, "The Start of Coworking."

[68] E. Mazareanu, "WeWork – Statistics & Facts," August 13, 2019, https://www.statista.com/topics/5086/wework/.

[69] US Census Bureau, "Geographic Area Series: Nonemployer Statistics for the US, States, Metropolitan Areas, and Counties," statistics for 2015 and 2016, *US Census Bureau*, June 21, 2018, https://factfinder.census.gov/faces/tableservices/jsf/pages/productview.xhtml?pid=NES_2016_00A2&prodType=table.

[70] Figures cited in Ilana DeBare, "Shared Work Spaces a Wave of the Future," *SFGate*, February 19, 2008, https://www.sfgate.com/bayarea/article/Shared-work-spaces-a-wave-of-the-future-3294193.php#item-85307-tbla-3. See also Carsten Foertsch, "What Is Coworking and Its Cultural Background?" October

office on a weekly or monthly basis.[71] This is about a shift in how we think about "space" when we are conducting the act of work, and the stimulus, benefits and experience that we feel we deserve. All this was forever changed by the microculture of coworking.

In the beginning, freelancers, one-person businesses and other independent workers used access to a regular communal workspace to enjoy the symbolic capital that comes with increased professional legitimacy and professional identity.[72] However, in order to function effectively, a professional space had to be married with a focus on community. Often referred to as the *"coworking movement,"* the fundamental idea is to create community among otherwise disparate workers, increase their networking opportunities, transform the routine and isolation of independent workers into a more social activity and, most importantly, bring people who allegedly share a core set of values together.[73] These aspects (engaging in collaboration, networking, building community around shared values, making work fun) are the forms of symbolic capital that people assign to coworking. They also serve as the perfect rationalization for choosing a coworking space when explaining this choice to others, in addition to factors like cost or convenience.

This community and shared set of values do not just shape the reason for joining; they also shape the way many coworking spaces are designed and where they are located. Almost all are built as an "open concept" but with access to private conference rooms and breakout

---

5, 2011. http://www.deskmag.com/en/what-is-coworking-about-the-changing-labor-market-208.

[71] The *Harvard Business Review* calls this the advantage of "spatial flexibility," a defining feature of coworking spaces. See Bacevice et al., "How Coworking Spaces Affect Employees' Professional Identities," *Harvard Business Review*, April 17, 2019, https://hbr.org/2019/04/how-coworking-spaces-affect-employees-professional-identities.

[72] Bacevice et al., "How Coworking Spaces Affect Professional Identities."

[73] DeBare, "Shared Work Spaces." That said, the community objectives of coworking spaces are typically undermined by the money-making character of a now major global industry. There is a vast literature on this topic. See, e.g., Sofia Ranchordás, "Does Sharing Mean Caring? Regulating Innovation in the Sharing Economy," *Minnesota Journal of Law, Science and Technology* 16, no. 1 (2015): 413–75.

rooms for phone calls. They are typically also located in prestigious or desirable locations in an urban center.

Last, in order to further promote a positive environment, they often have amenities such as fitness centers, lounge areas for socializing and unwinding with Ping-Pong tables and video games and kitchen spaces with perks like espresso machines and beer taps.

Compare this to the typical sea of cubicles that so many of us had to walk through in the 1990s and early 2000s, where workers were crammed together like cattle. All of a sudden, people who worked at coworking spaces had a litany of reasons for judging their work environment as superior. This not only raised employee expectations of work-related perks offered by start-ups; it also began and continues to have a significant influence on mainstream office design and marks a fundamental shift in the way office space is used.[74] A recent article titled "Coworking Disrupts Office Design" explains how the office market of more established companies has started to emulate the design and development features of coworking spaces, as they transform their traditional working environments from individual cubicles to a more open concept. They also increasingly forgo assigned desks and traditional corporate furniture.[75] Aimed especially at increasing productivity among so-called millennial employees, major companies such as PricewaterhouseCoopers (PwC), Apple, Google, Facebook, LinkedIn, GE and American Airlines have all committed to redesigning their corporate headquarters according to the coworking model.[76] "From wood-lined offices with pebbled glass doors to social spaces, open design and even dogs, traditional office is transforming to meet a new

---

[74] Paul Goodchild, "Coworking Disrupts Office Design," *Insight*, June 10, 2019, https://workplaceinsight.net/coworking-shaping-office-design-ways-might-think/; Matthew Rothstein, "Co-Working's Influence Is Now Everywhere in Office Space," *BISNOW*, January 8, 2018, https://www.bisnow.com/philadelphia/news/office/office-landlords-coworking-design-tenant-recruitment-83357; Cat Johnson, "Look Out, Coworking. Here Comes Big Money," *Shareable*, May 13, 2016, https://www.shareable.net/look-out-coworking-here-comes-big-money/.

[75] Goodchild, "Coworking Disrupts Office Design."

[76] Andrew Broadbent, "Why Big Corporations Are Moving into Coworking Spaces," *Entrepreneur*, January 22, 2018, https://web.archive.org/web/20180613161436/https://www.entrepreneur.com/article/307085.

generation of tenants—a generation, to some extent, that grew up with coworking."[77] Other major companies (e.g., Comcast, Microsoft, IBM) have also started renting out desks in coworking spaces so as to benefit from "the free-flowing idea environment" that they allegedly offer.[78]

Coworking spaces are a classic example of how a microculture can start out as a small movement and blossom into a mainstream norm that drives significant changes in a macroculture.

As we can see, the microculture of coworking and the cultural artifacts that define it are now starting to reshape the broader macroculture of work. But that is not all. The coworking microculture is also splintering into new and distinct microcultures. These include a microculture around "work-life balance"—with the emergence of more specific coworking models like New York City's Work and Play featuring onsite childcare and CoWorking with Wisdom, which combines shared office space with yoga, mindfulness and meditation, not surprisingly in Berkeley, California.[79] The *Harvard Business Review* also describes the emergence of coworking spaces geared at particular communities or demographics of people, such as women, people of color, social ventures, lawyers, architects and fashion businesses.[80]

We know something has reached mainstream status when it is satirized in pop culture. A 2019 episode of the HBO series *Broad City* pokes fun at start-up culture and coworking spaces, framing an entire episode around the concept. One of the show's protagonists, Ilana, who is eagerly seeking a new job in New York City, believes she is being interviewed for a position when, in actuality, she is simply being given a tour of a Manhattan coworking space that is ironically named YouWork. The scene opens with two men—the space's managers—trying

---

[77] Rothstein, "Co-Working's Influence Is Now Everywhere."

[78] Cited in Rothstein, "Co-Working's Influence Is Now Everywhere." See also Broadbent, "Why Big Corporations Are Moving into Coworking Spaces."

[79] See Ronda Kaysen, "Co-Working Spaces Add a Perk for Parents: Child Care," *New York Times*, December 23, 2016, https://www.nytimes.com/2016/12/23/realestate/co-working-spaces-add-a-perk-for-parents-child-care.html; and Nathan Chin, "CoWorking with Wisdom Opens in Downtown Berkeley," *Daily Californian*, July 19, 2018, https://www.dailycal.org/2018/07/19/coworking-wisdom-opens-downtown-berkeley-providing-space-work-life-balance/.

[80] Bacevice, "How Coworking Spaces Affect Employees' Professional Identities."

to sell the office's benefits to her by listing the perks of membership, such as a laid-back and convivial environment and free espresso, beer and snacks. Ilana is thrilled, assuming they are offering her a job rather than just the opportunity to pay rent for a desk.

Once she realizes what is happening, she protests by setting up her own "open air" coworking space, which she playfully names SheWork, targeted specifically at women who need a place to work but also want to smoke. She collects trash from the curb and creatively sets it up to look like office furniture, advertises charging ports (already offered for free by the city) and Wi-Fi (which she redirects, or steals, from the neighboring Starbucks), encourages smoking and charges fifty cents per minute. Hitting the nail on the head (especially regarding the commercial part of it), Ilana describes the coworking space model to her friend Abbi, who is a bit perplexed by the improvised operation: "All the great male entrepreneurs do it, OK? They take something that already exists, claim it was their idea, throw in some fancy furniture, and charge double for it!"[81]

The coworking space microculture, once a unique idea that had never existed, has transformed into a fundamental cultural artifact that shapes how we think about the spaces where we gather to work. As you look at your own category, can you think of a similar example? Did something "change the game" and if so, where did it start? Were you able to recognize the threat it posed to your business before it was too late?

Of course, microcultures are not always a brand new game changer. Sometimes, they are a well-known concept that is co-opted to change the very meaning of something in culture. And perhaps you are carrying one right now.

Microculture Characteristic #2: A New Interpretation of an Old Idea

The second characteristic that we might see in a microculture is that *consumers interpret a broadly known concept in a new way*, which then

---

[81] Abbi Jacobson, dir., *Broad City*, season 5, episode 2, "SheWork and S*** Bucket," aired January 31, 2019, on HBO.

changes the marketplace. Unlike our coworking space example, where a completely new approach was introduced to the market, here the microculture co-opts and redefines a relatively well-established idea. Think about how fat was transformed when a group of consumers started to identify the health benefits of "good fat" versus "bad fat." The interpretation of fat as a whole was redefined over time.

Now imagine that we did the same for the concept of "leather."

What? You haven't heard about "vegan leather"? It's changing the face of high-end fashion accessories. It is still in its nascency and, despite the term "leather" being loaded with symbolic capital, "vegan leather" has succeeded in becoming a microculture that borrows the broadly known concept of "leather" and turns it on its head.

I know what you are saying. Aren't you talking about "pleather"?

Yes. And no. Consider that the ultimate authority in high fashion trends, *Vogue* magazine, recently wrote that "eco-conscious fashion is creeping into our collective consciousness, opening the door for a host of enterprising ethical and sustainable bag brands."[82] Also consider that this year (2019) saw the first ever Vegan Fashion Week in LA.[83] The event's organizer (Emmanuelle Rienda) strove to redefine the concept of veganism via fashion, stating that: "'Now is the time to create a Fashion Week that shows how being vegan today is not only about animals—it's about being good to all beings on the planet, humans included. It's not a matter of style anymore. It's a matter of choice.'"[84]

Vegan leather is not a material. It's a movement.

In another issue of Vogue, a fashion influencer writes, "equally as good-looking—and often more affordable—than their designer leather cousins, vegan-friendly handbags are a wise investment."[85]

---

[82] Giorgina Ramazzotti, "The Luxury Eco Bags That Are Good for Your Wardrobe and Your Conscience," *Vogue*, November 9, 2018, https://www.vogue.co.uk/gallery/best-eco-bags.

[83] Emily Farra, "Vegan Fashion Week Is Coming to L.A.—And It's About a Lot More Than Eco Leather and Faux Fur," *Vogue*, January 14, 2019, https://www.vogue.com/article/vegan-fashion-week-los-angeles-emmanuelle-rienda.

[84] Farra, "Vegan Fashion Week."

[85] Giorgina Ramazzotti, "Vegan Faux Leather Bags That Look as Good as the Real Thing," *Vogue*, November 29, 2018, https://www.vogue.co.uk/gallery/best-vegan-bags.

Of course, affordable is a relative term. Stella McCartney's red vegan tote bag sells for about $980. But despite the price tag, McCartney has driven tremendous growth in the vegan luxury fashion market by introducing vegan leather shoes and handbags.

But wait. Pleather was invented in 1963. And if Stella McCartney has been selling ethical brands since 2013, why is this "new crop of emerging ethical brands"[86] starting to grow in popularity now? Likely because the "vegan leather" microculture is being pulled into the mainstream by the macroculture of veganism as a whole. Previously regarded as a domain of radical politics, personal sacrifice and harsh judgment of those not willing to give up animal-based products, veganism has undergone a major cultural shift. Triggered in part by a series of wildly successful environmentally themed and rather polemical documentaries on Netflix (e.g., *Cowspiracy*, 2014, whose executive director was Leonardo DiCaprio), mass audiences are getting the message that animal agriculture (in particular cattle farming) is the central culprit in the escalating global climate crisis.[87] Veganism has gone from fringe movement to mainstream, largely thanks to a transformation driven by the movement rebranding itself. As stated in the *Guardian*: "People feel empowered, it doesn't feel like a sacrifice [anymore]. That's a huge shift. Whereas before, veganism may have been viewed like you were giving up something, now it's been reframed as what you gain: you gain health, you gain a greater sense of living in bounds with your values, you gain all the environmental benefits."[88]

In the US, the sales of plant-based foods experienced rapid growth in 2018. Compared to the previous year, the market saw plant-based meat alternatives grow by 24% while "other dairy alternatives" grew

---

[86] Ramazzotti, "Vegan Faux Leather Bags."

[87] Dan Hancox, "The Unstoppable Rise of Veganism: How a Fringe Movement Went Mainstream," *Guardian*. April 1, 2018, https://www.theguardian.com/lifeandstyle/2018/apr/01/vegans-are-coming-millennials-health-climate-change-animal-welfare.

[88] Hancox, "The Unstoppable Rise of Veganism."

by 50%.[89] At its core, the plant-based lifestyle movement is driven by concerns for animal welfare, the environment and personal health.

Now, in 2019, we see the fashion industry, which is repurposing long-standing faux-leather products (the aforementioned pleather, vinyl-based accessories and other plastic knockoffs of leather) while creating a new microculture under the "vegan leather" label. This is not a new idea or new concept. On the contrary, an old material (pleather) and old label (leather) are co-opted to redefine the definition and the symbolic capital associated with both.

Pleather was cheap and lacked quality. Vegan leather, on the other hand, replicates the texture and appearance of real leather while also eliminating animal cruelty and minimizing the use of environmentally toxic substances such as fossil fuels.

Was the popularity of older faux-leather or pleather products partly defined by a concern with animal welfare? Somewhat. But it was not linked to concerns with environmental sustainability. Pleather was almost entirely linked to a value proposition, in that it provided consumers with access to low-cost products from fast-fashion labels rather than luxury brands.

Compared to its predecessors, the new vegan leather fashion label carries status and cachet.

That is what retailers are hoping to communicate anyway. "With the term 'vegan leather,' manufacturers and retailers have tried to piggyback off the image of well-heeled shoppers who browse farmer's markets and Whole Foods."[90] The burgeoning vegan leather industry is appealing to consumers by trying to tap into the three symbolic meanings defining the macroculture of veganism: animal welfare, environmental sustainability and personal health. As a result, efforts are underway to comply with the consumer demand for ethical and environmentally conscious vegan leather products. This has given rise

---

[89] Gallup poll findings cited in Jan Conway, "Consumers Who Are Vegan or Vegetarian in the U.S. 2018, by Age Group," *Statista*, August 9, 2019, https://www.statista.com/statistics/738851/vegan-vegetarian-consumers-us/.

[90] Shan Li, "Vegan Fashion Grows More Fashionable as Textile Technology Improves," *Los Angeles Times*, February 4, 2015, https://www.latimes.com/business/la-fi-vegan-fashion-20150205-story.html.

to a high-end luxury market around new vegan leather accessories whose prices are in part justified by their use of "lab-grown leather" or other products that are derived from scientific experimentation with plant-based materials (e.g., cork, pineapple leaves, mushroom mycelium and even kombucha). These materials will ideally replace leather hides and plastics entirely.[91] However, while some brands are indeed trying to shift away from traditionally polluting leather alternatives, we're still "some way off" from an eco-friendly substitute that doesn't harm animals or the environment.[92]

A fashion coordinator from the animal rights group People for the Ethical Treatment of Animals (PETA), Christina Sewell, succinctly sums up the intersection of meanings around the emergence of the vegan leather trend, stating that consumers tend to "identify vegans with a little bit higher class of people who really care about the environment and animals ... We want to show that being cruelty-free doesn't mean wearing a hemp bag over your head ... What better term to use than vegan? Unlike faux leather, which sounds kind of cheap."[93] The symbolic capital and status that derives from the emergent microculture around vegan leather is simultaneously about a concern for animal welfare, the environment and high-end fashion. We might also consider how these three meanings are in tension with one another as the vegan leather trend continues to mature.

As the microculture of vegan leather moves increasingly into the mainstream, we can expect to see an increase of fast-fashion labels— that is, not just high-end luxury ones—offering products that they claim are ethical and socially conscious. Mass-market retailers such as Dr Martens, Top Shop and Marks & Spencers all introduced vegan leather footwear in 2019, while H&M launched a collection made with

[91] Tegan Taylor, "Is 'Vegan Leather' a Sustainable Alternative to Animal Leather?" *Australian Broadcasting Corporation (ABC)*, last modified May 24, 2018, https://www.abc.net.au/news/science/2018-05-24/vegan-leather-is-it-a-sustainable-alternative/9774768.

[92] Alder Wicker, "Fashion's Long Hunt for the Perfect Vegan Leather," *Vogue*, June 17, 2019, https://www.voguebusiness.com/technology/vegan-faux-leather-stella-mccartney-prada-versace.

[93] Cited in Li, "Vegan Fashion Grows More Fashionable."

vegan pineapple leather and orange silk in the same year; the year of vegan fashion.[94] Clearly, the vegan leather microculture is changing the concept of what constitutes quality in the fashion industry. And as we will see in the next example, a microculture can also change the very habits and rituals that we carry out in our daily lives.

Microculture Characteristic #3: New Rituals Getting Normalized

The third identifier of microcultures involves the *formation of new habits or rituals around consumption.* Unlike the first characteristic, which is about introducing a completely new idea, this characteristic is about new rituals that are placed into an existing context. To better understand the difference, let's consider for a moment how the coworking space was born out of the idea of making more professional work settings more accessible. This started with a "patient zero"—a person with an idea birthed a concept, and the idea blossomed and spread.

But what if you can't pinpoint "patient zero"? Or, in the case of the following example, "hipster zero." What if a population of consumers starts to change the way they do something in order to gain symbolic capital by differentiating themselves from others? Like a generation of men who chose to grow beards and unknowingly transformed the men's grooming industry?

In 2017, the global male grooming products market reached a value of $57.7 billion.[95] This whopping industry value is particularly

---

[94] Ellie Pithers, "The Leather Debate: Is Vegan Leather a Sustainable Alternative to the Real Thing?" *Vogue,* April 24, 2019, https://www.vogue.co.uk/article/vegan-leather-sustainability-debate-2019; Sascha Camilli, "H&M Launches Collection Made with Vegan Pineapple Leather and Orange Silk," *Plant Based News (PBN)* April 1, 2019, https://www.plantbasednews.org/lifestyle/h-m-collection-vegan-pineappple-leather-orange-silk.

[95] BusinessWire, "Global Male Grooming Products Market 2018–2023," *BusinessWire,* September 10, 2018, https://www.businesswire.com/news/home/20180910005394/en/Global-Male-Grooming-Products-Market-2018-2023—.

impressive because until just about two decades ago, male grooming was pretty much limited to the basics—shaving cream, deodorant, aftershave and shampoo. Men who wanted more could only really pick up products from the women's cosmetics aisle at the drugstore or pilfer something from their wives', girlfriends', moms' or sisters' cosmetic stash. But that has since changed. *Drastically.* Today, male grooming entails a myriad of products, including male-specific skincare products like moisturizers, facial creams, cleansers and scrubs (marketed as a product distinct from women's exfoliants), bronzers, concealers, serums, face masks, anti-aging products and even makeup (rebranded as "warpaint"), such as the playfully renamed *manliner* to refer to eyeliner made specially for men.[96] Store-based retailers, including major department stores such as Macy's, Bloomingdale's and Nordstrom, have redesigned stores to include distinct sections for men's grooming products.[97] Target is also getting into the game as it "manscapes its male grooming business," adding male-specific grooming products to its private Goodfellows label and creating separate sections in their stores for male grooming products.[98] A January 2019 article in the *Chicago Tribune* explains why sports legends like Michael Jordan, Shaquille O'Neal and numerous other NBA players "love pedicures."[99]

---

[96] BusinessWire, "Global Male Grooming Products Market 2018–2023"; see also Lauren Valenti, "The History of Guyliner," *Marie Claire*, July 10, 2015, https://www.marieclaire.com/beauty/news/g3035/men-wearing-eyeliner-history/.

[97] Orbis Research, "Men's Grooming Products Market Rising Popularity in 2019, Global Insights, Key Developments of Products, Top Brands (Beiersdorf, Kroger) and Forecast Till 2023," *Reuters*, October 4, 2018, https://www.reuters.com/brandfeatures/venture-capital/article?id=56764.

[98] Global Cosmetic Industry, "Target Manscapes Its Male Grooming Business," *Global Cosmetic Industry*, August 29, 2018, https://www.gcimagazine.com/marketstrends/consumers/men/Target-Manscapes-Its-Male-Grooming-Business—492016111.html; see also Cara Salpini, "Target's Goodfellow Private Label Moves into Men's Grooming," *RetailDive*, May 20, 2019, https://www.retaildive.com/news/targets-goodfellow-private-label-moves-into-mens-grooming/555145/.

[99] Nate Robinson, "If It's Good Enough for Michael Jordan and Shaq...: Why NBA Players Love Pedicures," *Chicago Tribune*, January 15, 2019, https://www.chicagotribune.com/sports/ct-nba-players-pedicures-20190115-story.html.

What brought on this change? When we look at the current trend, it should come as no surprise that the rise of men's grooming is attributable first and foremost to social media: "There is an increasing use of the Internet for grooming tips, which has further resulted in an increase in the number of grooming blogs and websites. Moreover, websites dedicated to men's grooming products have become popular as a result of increasing demand for such products."[100] In our online "selfie" generation, appearance—and its around-the-clock maintenance—is important to everyone, irrespective of gender. What better evidence of this than social media influencers like James Charles, the teenage makeup artist and Instagram celebrity (he currently has 15.7 million Instagram followers) who is known for his chiseled cheekbones and extra-long eyelashes and is having a major impact on the male grooming industry, especially on a younger generation of new consumers? In 2016, CoverGirl chose James Charles as its first ever *male* CoverGirl spokesmodel, referring to him as the industry's one and only "coverboy" as he became the face and lashes of the brand's new mascara "So Lashy!"[101]

This flourishing microculture around men's grooming dates back to the early aughts, more specifically the year 2002 when Mark Simpson, an influential gay male writer, published an article in *Slate* magazine titled: "Meet the Metrosexual: He's Well Dressed, Narcissistic and Obsessed with Butts. But Don't Call Him Gay." In the article, Simpson defined the typical metrosexual as "a young man with money to spend, living in or within the easy reach of a metropolis— because that's where all the best shops, clubs, gyms and hairdressers are."[102] He referred to British soccer player David Beckham as the icon of metrosexuality: although Beckham painted his fingernails

[100] Orbis Research, "Men's Grooming Products Market Rising Popularity"; see also BusinessWire, "Global Male Grooming Products Market 2018–2023."

[101] Carly Cardellino, "CoverGirl Announces Its First Male CoverGirl Spokesmodel," *Marie Claire*, October 11, 2016, https://www.marieclaire.com/beauty/a23038/male-covergirl-james-charles/.

[102] Mark Simpson, "Meet the Metrosexual: He's Well Dressed, Narcissistic and Obsessed with Butts. But Don't Call Him Gay," *Slate* July 22, 2002, https://www.salon.com/test/2002/07/22/metrosexual/.

and braided his hair, he nevertheless exhibited strength and prowess (i.e., traditional heterosexual masculinity) on the soccer field.[103] In short, the metrosexual was a man concerned with his appearance but masculine enough in other ways to comfortably partake in feminized consumer habits.

A year later, another major piece on metrosexuals appeared, this time in the *New York Times* and with the title "Metrosexuals Come Out." At this point, the term and its implications had already become a mainstream component of public discourse, especially in consumer culture. The microculture of men's grooming was pushing forward, influenced strongly by mass media and entertainment presenting a more expansive interpretation of masculinity to general audiences. Around the same time, in 2003, the Bravo channel launched *Queer Eye for the Straight Guy*. This was a reality TV show that featured the Fab Five, a group of stylish and urbane gay men, traveling around the US to give clueless straight men a makeover or what they called a "make-better" so as to transform them "from drab to fab," as per the show's motto. The series was a wild success for five seasons and was revived in 2018 by Netflix with an updated version. Not coincidentally, 2003 was also the year that saw the introduction of the word "manscaping" into the English lexicon. Defined as "the trimming or shaving of a man's body hair so as to enhance his appearance," it generally refers more specifically to dealing with hair below the neckline through shaving or waxing.[104] Cultural analysts have attributed the rise of male-only spas, manicures and pedicures for men and waxing services for men's "manscaping" needs to the popularity of shows like *Queer Eye for the Straight Guy*, which first made it socially permissible for men to engage in activities that had previously been limited to women.[105]

---

[103] Warren St. John, "Metrosexuals Comes Out," *New York Times*, June 22, 2003, https://www.nytimes.com/2003/06/22/style/metrosexuals-come-out.html.

[104] Merriam Webster's Dictionary: https://www.merriam-webster.com/dictionary/manscaping.

[105] Kyra Kyles, "Now Serving: Beefcake," *Chicago Tribune*, November 15, 2005, https://www.chicagotribune.com/news/ct-xpm-2005-11-15-0511150317-story.html.

The era of the metrosexual may not have lasted all that long, but its impact on popular and consumer culture was significant. By the end of the aughts, the microculture of men's grooming that revolved around the clean-shaven, fashion-savvy metrosexual suddenly got competition from a new male type, the rugged and manly lumbersexual: "young urban men were swapping out post-shave ointments and chest baring V-necks [the domain of metrosexuals] for Grizzly Adams beards and plaid flannel shirts—[it was] a celebration of old-school masculinity."[106] New meanings (and consumer habits) were thus continuing to take shape into the new decade. By 2013, men spent more on male-specific toiletries than on shaving products for the first time ever.[107]

A *Vice* magazine article succinctly sums up the pop-culture-defined distinction—and clash—between metrosexuals and lumbersexuals: while the former group believed in industry and mass production, the latter group was driven by an anti-industry, pro-local and handmade ethos.[108] Either way, both types have helped push the current microculture of men's grooming into the mainstream. While metrosexuals may have driven male-specific product development in mass-market brands such as Nivea (Men Active Energy series), Dove (Men+Care), L'Oréal (Men Expert Line), and Estée Lauder (Lab Series Skincare for Men),[109] lumbersexuals can be linked to the burgeoning of smaller, high-end male-specific labels and, significantly, to the ever-growing men's grooming microculture around beards. A multi-billion-dollar industry in its own right—led by Mo Bro's in the UK and Beardbrand in the US—"beard mania" has given rise to a whole range

---

[106] Alex Williams, "'Metrosexuals' Were Just Straight Men Who Loved Self-Care. Right?" *New York Times*, June 15, 2018, https://www.nytimes.com/2018/06/15/style/metrosexuals.html.

[107] Walker in Global Cosmetic Industry, 2014.

[108] Vice Staff. 2016, "Whatever Happened to Metrosexuals?" *Vice*, June 6, 2016, https://www.vice.com/en_ca/article/3bjyek/whatever-happened-to-the-metrosexuals-324.

[109] Marketplace, "How It Became OK for Guys to Take Care of Themselves," *Marketplace* podcast, January 6, 2016, https://www.marketplace.org/2016/01/05/world/how-it-became-ok-guys-take-care-themselves/; Orbis Research, "Men's Grooming Products Market Rising Popularity."

of beard-specific products such as beard brushes, creams and oils, high-quality razors and electric trimmers, beard dye and, of course, high-end (or "hipster") barber shops.[110]

The move of the men's grooming microculture into the mainstream has gone hand in hand with the creation of new definitions of masculinity, be it metrosexual or lumbersexual, which are then used for the marketing of new kinds of male-specific products. In her ethnography of male salons titled *Styling Masculinity: Gender, Class, and Inequality in the Men's Grooming Industry*, sociologist Kristy Barber makes the argument that men's grooming is not strictly about beauty or appearance but about a particular ideal of masculinity that is driven by white, straight and wealthy urban professionals who have turned male grooming into a multi-billion-dollar industry.[111]

For our purposes, this is another way of saying that the growing microculture around men's grooming is driven by ever-shifting notions around what it means to be a man in contemporary society. The #MeToo movement, for example, started in late 2017 and may have ushered in yet another kind of masculinity, creating new meanings that media outlets refer to as "softer masculinity" that challenge stereotypes associated with traditional masculinity (e.g., rough, brutish, threatened by associations with femininity). Major brands like Gillette, Dove and Axe have all put out ads in the last couple of years that have sought to expand the definition of masculinity by showing sensitive men involved in self-care, committed to being a

---

[110] John D. Moore, "Lumbersexual Look: A Manly Guide to Rugged Style and Grooming," *Guy Counseling*, February 22, 2017, https://guycounseling.com/lumbersexual-look-style-grooming-guide/; see also the Inside the Marketplace, "Why the Beard Grooming Market Continues To Grow," *Inside the Marketplace*, August 16, 2018, http://insidethemarketplace.com/2018/08/16/why-the-beard-market-continues-to-grow/; Richard E. Ocejo, *Masters of Craft: Old Jobs in the New Urban Economy* (Princeton, NJ: Princeton University Press, 2017).

[111] One of the main arguments in her book is also that women remain predominantly responsible for the labor required by men to perform *both* their grooming rituals (as hairstylists, estheticians who do waxing, eyebrow plucking, facials, manicures and pedicures in high-end men's salons) *and* help reassure them of their (privileged hetero) masculinity in the process.

good and present dad and opposing sexism, sexual harassment and bullying.[112]

As the microculture of male grooming continues to move forward, the change in the ritual of grooming continues to *assert its dominance in the grooming (or beauty) macroculture*. The needs of male consumers are beginning to approximate those of the traditionally female-led core market in the broader grooming (or beauty) industry. For example, new microcultures around natural and organic products are exerting just as much pressure on men's grooming as they are (or recently were) in the industry of women's cosmetics, beauty and body care.[113] As explained on the *Cosmetics Business* website, "Men's wellness and personal care is catching up much quicker with product trends in the women's space, *so it's worth not considering the two to be necessarily separate any more*. As such, trends like vegan, clean, halal, natural and farm-to-face, if they are not already, will become quickly wrapped in to men's personal care and wellness."[114]

While beards have grown both on people's faces and in popularity, the change in ritual has transformed not just how men present themselves but also how they want to be perceived in this world. They have used their body to challenge perceptions of masculinity and in the process have normalized habits and rituals that would have typically been ostracized or made fun of in the masculine culture of the past.

---

[112] Hazel Cills, "A Short History of Manly Beauty Products for Masculine Men," *Jezebel*, June 19, 2019, https://jezebel.com/a-short-history-of-manly-beauty-products-for-masculine-1834956610; Matt Krupnick, "Ad Campaigns Tag Along as Men Embrace Different Paths," *New York Times*, June 4, 2017, https://www.nytimes.com/2017/06/04/business/media/advertising-masculinity.html.

[113] Orbis Research, "Men's Grooming Products Market Rising Popularity" (emphasis added).

[114] Cosmetics Business, "Cosmetics Business Reveals the Top 5 Trends Disrupting Men's Care in New Report," *Cosmetics Business*, April 10, 2019, https://www.cosmeticsbusiness.com/news/article_page/Cosmetics_Business_reveals_the_top_5_trends_disrupting_mens_care_in_new_report/153663 (emphasis added).

Microculture Characteristic #4: Structural Shifts

The fourth characteristic has to do with the *breakdown of unique structural compositions*, that is, when certain cultural practices or behaviors that are considered to be the domain of a certain class of people are suddenly taken over by a different class of people.

This can clearly be seen in the rise of comfort food in haute cuisine. More and more, chefs are taking traditionally "lowbrow" items and inserting them into "highbrow" cultural practices. Consider how often we are seeing working-class foods like mac 'n' cheese, burgers, meatloaf and hot dogs finding their way onto high-end restaurant menus at a premium price. Gourmet food magazines write about the joy of "authentic" foods that can be transformed into a "high status dish" by adding particular ingredients (truffle oil, specialty mushrooms, homemade sourdough buns, foie gras, etc.) or by preparing them in a particular way (e.g., in your homemade clay oven). This microculture will serve as the perfect example of a unique structural composition coming apart. But first, let's understand the reason for this particular movement in culture.

When one starts to think about the cultural impact of the 2008 financial crisis, *"increased* commercialization in foodie culture" probably doesn't jump to mind.

But it happened. Following the financial fallout, foods and eating practices that were once considered lowbrow or working class were suddenly being celebrated as gourmet.[115] Before this shift, being a "foodie" was quite exclusive. First coined in the mid-1980s by Ann Barr and Paul Levy in their book *The Official Foodie Handbook*, foodies were described as "hobbyists with a keen interest in the sourcing, preparation, presentation, consumption and discussion of food."[116] The only thing missing from this description is that gourmet and

---

[115] Josephine Livingstone, "What Was the Foodie?" *New Republic*, March 18, 2019, https://newrepublic.com/article/153335/foodie; Josee Johnston and Shyon Baumann, *Foodies: Democracy and Distinction in the Gourmet Foodscape*, 2nd ed. (New York and London: Routledge, 2015).

[116] Jennifer Benjamin, "Foodie Culture and Its Impact on the Culinary Landscape," *Lightspeed HQ*, last modified June 23, 2016, https://www.lightspeedhq.com/blog/foodie-culture-impact/.

foodie culture had one key requirement: money to access it. And up to 2008, being a foodie or lover of gourmet food was a strong indication of wealth.

But in light of a massive financial shockwave, *a new microculture around working-class gourmet food (or gourmet comfort food)* emerged. And "restaurants started capitalizing on shows of austerity."[117] In other words, the economic crisis made consumers averse to showing off wealth (whether or not they had it) and created nostalgia for (usually imagined) "authenticity" and a rustic or peasant style of cooking. Symbolic capital was now swarming around displays of frugality or at least things associated with spending less money.

But were people actually spending less money? No. Do we spend less now, more than a decade later? No. In fact, millennials are spending more money dining out or ordering in than any generation before them.[118] What has changed are the *meanings* around eating and purchasing food. A staff writer at the *New Republic*, herself a millennial, explains it this way: "Much of millennial consumer culture is about our instinctive sense of precarity, our allergy to corporate signifiers, and our formless urge to be good people who won't screw up the world all over again. But the food market adapted, of course, and continued to take our money, though selling us different values. Transparency, authenticity, good health, convenience, anti-snobbery."[119] People were still spending loads of money on food, but increasingly on food that exhibited the values mentioned above.

The nose-to-tail trend that emerged in the early 2010s is an example of this. Suddenly, the meanings and symbolic capital around historically the cheapest and un-sexiest of food options—in mainstream (white) US food culture anyway—namely, pig entrails, cow hearts, lamb tongue, and other innards and organ meats were recast almost concurrently as "fine food," "natural," "authentic rustic

---

[117] Livingstone, "What Was the Foodie?"
[118] Alexandra Talty, "New Study Finds Millennials Spend 44 Percent of Food Dollars on Eating Out," *Forbes*, October 17, 2016, https://www.forbes.com/sites/alexandratalty/2016/10/17/millennials-spend-44-percent-of-food-dollars-on-eating-out-says-food-institute/#f45a94e3ff68.
[119] Livingstone, "What Was the Foodie?"

cuisine" and "adventurous fare." What was once considered "gross" now had cachet and could earn farmers extra money, whereas they had previously been throwing it away (for lack of a market). A 2018 *Wall Street Journal* article asks in its title: "Barbecued Beef Heart Anyone?"; it then answers its own question by declaring that "Offal Enjoys Its Foodie Moment."[120]

There are numerous other examples of traditionally working-class foods or eating habits that have been taken up by middle- or upper-class echelons of society.[121] One only needs to look at the popularity of gourmet food trucks to see how this trend has played out. Historically used as cheap and quick lunch spots for blue-collar workers at factories and construction sites, they have since been rebranded as "gourmet" food destinations. The first of such food trucks, Kogi, is said to have been started by chef Roy Choi in LA in 2008.[122] A few months later, a *New York* magazine article described how the food truck has "largely transcended its roach-coach classification and is now a respectable venue for aspiring chefs to launch careers."[123] The taco food truck in particular is "the new gourmet temple," according to a *Smithsonian* magazine interview with culinary authority and adventurer Anthony Bourdain from 2014.[124]

Of course, the microculture around working-class gourmet foods is also being shaped by competing microcultures concerned with environmental sustainability, animal welfare and human health

---

[120] Benjamin Parkin, "Barbecued Beef Heart Anyone? Offal Enjoys Its Foodie Moment," *Wall Street Journal*, September 6, 2018, https://www.wsj.com/articles/barbecued-beef-heart-anyone-offal-enjoys-its-foodie-moment-1536243262.

[121] Josee Johnston and Shyon Baumann, "Democracy versus Distinction: A Study of Omnivorousness in Gourmet Food Writing," *American Journal of Sociology* 113 (2007): 165–204.

[122] Lorri Mealey, "A History of the Food Truck: The Rise of the Food Truck Culture," *The Balance Small Business*, last modified October 14, 2019, https://www.thebalancesmb.com/a-history-of-food-trucks-2888314.

[123] Bryant Urstadt, "Intentionally Temporary," *New York Magazine*, September 11, 2009, http://nymag.com/shopping/features/58998/.

[124] Ron Rosenbaum, "Anthony Bourdain's Theory on the Foodie Revolution," *Smithsonian*, July 14, 2014, https://www.smithsonianmag.com/arts-culture/anthony-bourdains-theory-foodie-revolution-180951848/.

(much like the vegan leather trend discussed in an earlier section)[125]—leading to increases in the sales of local and/or organic foods, the rejection of animal-based proteins and a return to homemade or homegrown foods.

As seen in the previous characteristics, consumers are looking to tell the world something about themselves with the things they buy, and especially with the food they eat. Symbolic capital is captured as they challenge class expectations and show themselves to be authentic and responsible consumers.

Microculture Characteristic #5: Breaking Down Barriers

The fifth and final characteristic that a microculture may exhibit is what we refer to as *economic stratification*. We can think of this as the flipside of characteristic #4. This feature of microcultures is about democratizing access to services or goods that were previously limited to only a handful of wealthy consumers.

Consider the rise of bespoke suits (and especially companies such as Indochino). These used to be accessible to only the wealthiest of people but are now made more readily available to a much larger portion of the population through online purveyors. Or, as we will dissect below, consider the rise of the sharing economy, with websites such as Airbnb, now a $38 billion company. This new offering in the travel category has led to the creation of solutions that have made activities and experiences that were once reserved for the elite more economically accessible to the broader population.[126] It also serves as an example of a highly flexible economic network.

In its most basic form, the sharing economy involves sharing services or resources with strangers. Buyer and seller are directly

---

[125] Lucy King, "It's 2016 and We've Reached Peak Food Culture," *Vice*, June 27, 2016, https://www.vice.com/en_au/article/8g3mgp/its-2016-and-weve-reached-peak-food-culture.

[126] Dina Gerdeman, "The Airbnb Effect: Cheaper Rooms for Travelers, Less Revenue for Hotels," *Forbes*, February 27, 2018, https://www.forbes.com/sites/hbsworkingknowledge/2018/02/27/the-airbnb-effect-cheaper-rooms-for-travelers-less-revenue-for-hotels/#7393ab92d672.

connected via the Internet (which theoretically eliminates the need for a corporate middleman). Consider eBay, the online auction and shopping website, which triggered the birth of the sharing economy back in 1995.[127] But the sharing economy as a whole didn't break into the mainstream until 2011, at which point *TIME* magazine dubbed it one of the "Ten Ideas That Will Change the World."[128]

Today, the sharing economy, which is also known as shareconomy, collaborative economy, collaborative consumption, peer-to-peer economy and relationship economy, is projected to grow to $335 billion by 2025 from $15 billion in 2014, according to *Forbes* magazine.[129] It has developed hand in hand with peer-to-peer (P2P) technology, as strangers connect via digital platforms—usually apps—to negotiate the terms of accessing underutilized assets, be it cars, homes, garage spaces, office spaces (coworking spaces, like many of the examples offered here, exhibit multiple microculture characteristics), and so on.[130]

Big data is also fundamental to the sharing economy, as it allows for more online information about people and things or places that are available for "hire."[131] The sharing economy moreover emerged as a result of the pain points created by the economic crash of 2008, when people were dealing with serious financial difficulties and forced

[127] Association of MBAs, "The March of the Sharing Economy," *Association of MBAs*, February 15, 2019, https://www.mbaworld.com/blogs-and-articles/the-march-of-the-sharing-economy.

[128] Brian Walsh, "10 Ideas That Will Change the World," *Time*, March 17, 2011, http://content.time.com/time/specials/packages/article/0,28804,2059521 2059717 2059710,00.html.

[129] Sarote Tabcum Jr., "The Sharing Economy Is Still Growing, and Businesses Should Take Note," *Forbes*, March 4, 2019, https://www.forbes.com/sites/forbeslacouncil/2019/03/04/the-sharing-economy-is-still-growing-and-businesses-should-take-note/#7bed100d4c33.

[130] Michael A. Cusumano, "The Sharing Economy Meets Reality," *Communications of the ACM* 61, no. 1 (2018): 26–28, https://cacm.acm.org/magazines/2018/1/223874-the-sharing-economy-meets-reality/abstract.

[131] Economist, "The Rise of the Sharing Economy," *Economist*, March 9, 2013, https://www.economist.com/news/leaders/21573104-internet-everything-hire-rise-sharing-economy.

to seek out alternative solutions for getting by. It gave struggling consumers the chance to become vendors or providers of unused assets they already owned, with basically no overhead cost and on a flexible basis.[132] It also gave them the opportunity to access certain goods and services that they otherwise would not be as readily able to afford. The microculture of the sharing economy is thus defined by several meanings, including trust, scarcity, economic advantage and, of course, the sharing or exchange of assets or resources. But the sharing economy also sits in a macroculture that is ultimately about profit and commercialization. Let's see how this works.

The sharing economy consists of two different business models, both of which are about gaining *access* to a good (or service) as opposed to ownership of it. In the first, assets (or services) are *individually* owned or offered (as in the case of Airbnb, Lyft, Uber, etc.) and "rented out" to consumers for a limited period of time. This model is considered a completely new type of business model (and thus also reflective of the first characteristic of microculture, the introduction of an entirely new idea). In the second model, assets in the sharing economy are owned by a *company* and lent out for a limited period of time (e.g., Zipcar owned by Avis, Car2Go owned by Daimler AG, city-bike shares or e-scooter companies). This model is not new in and of itself but is rather a modified *version* of a traditional rental business (and so, also reflective of characteristic #2, the reinterpretation of a known concept).[133]

Airbnb is probably the most famous example of the sharing economy and has markedly democratized tourism by making accommodations cheaper and more plentiful. The original idea was based on couch surfing, which functioned according to an agreement of personal exchange: a host would allow a stranger to sleep on their couch for free with the expectation that they might one day visit the stranger's city and sleep on their couch for free. Airbnb monetized

---

[132] Steve Henn, "What's Mine Is Yours (for a Price) in the Sharing Economy," *National Public Radio (NPR)*, November 13, 2013, https://www.npr.org/sections/alltechconsidered/2013/11/13/244860511/whats-mine-is-yours-for-a-price-in-the-sharing-economy.

[133] Cusumano, "The Sharing Economy Meets Reality."

this idea but maintained the principle of affordable accommodation by making use of a local host's spare bedroom or mattress/couch. The company started out as AirBed & Breakfast in 2008 in San Francisco when its founders, Brian Chesky and Joe Gebbia, realized that people who were attending the Industrial Design Conference could not find accommodation in the city's saturated rental and hotel market. They set up air mattresses in their own apartments, offered homemade breakfast and charged a fee. They began as a really small-scale operation: just a couple of guys with an idea about how to deal with the saturated rental/accommodation market in San Francisco and some other nearby towns. They targeted high-profile events in places where attendees would likely have trouble finding (affordable) lodging in more conventional accommodation spaces like hotels.

By 2009, the online company had changed its name to the shorter and catchier Airbnb and expanded to include a greater variety of properties, like entire apartments and houses, private rooms, castles, boats, manors, tree houses, igloos and even private islands.[134] Airbnb then isn't necessarily just about a more affordable service being offered to a broader range of consumers but also broadens the landscape of options available to tourists beyond conventional hotel rooms, while also influencing where and how they travel: "Consumers don't always pay a lower price … What changes is the quality of the listings. You might find a Fifth Avenue apartment or a place by the beach at a more reasonable price than you would if Airbnb wasn't an option. Or a listing might have additional amenities, like a kitchen."[135]

As of 2018, the company had lodging options across 81,000 cities in 192 countries worldwide and an estimated worth of at least $38 billion.[136] It should thus come as no surprise that *the sharing*

---

[134] Martin Luenendonk, "Airbnb – Strategies for Renting Your Accomodation [sic] Online," *Cleverism*, November 19, 2014, https://www.cleverism.com/airbnb-strategies-selling-products-online/.

[135] Gerdeman, "The Airbnb Effect."

[136] Trefis Team, "As a Rare Profitable Unicorn, Airbnb Appears to Be Worth at Least $38 Billion," *Forbes*, May, 11 2018, https://www.forbes.com/sites/greatspeculations/2018/05/11/as-a-rare-profitable-unicorn-airbnb-appears-to-be-worth-at-least-38-billion/#148ea6452741.

economy microculture around Airbnb now dominates the mainstream and has driven significant change in various macrocultures almost simultaneously: the hotel/lodging industry, the tourism industry and the housing rental market.[137] For example, while conventional hotels tend to be located in specifically designated "tourist areas" (or near airports and bus and train stations), Airbnb offers tourists the chance to rent accommodations in neighborhoods where people actually live. Sometimes, users can build meaningful relationships with their hosts. While the company promotes this more "authentic" experience of travel as a major advantage, local residents and housing activists the world over see this as more of a nuisance or even a complete disruption of residential life and the housing market. An April 2019 article in *The New Yorker*, titled "The Airbnb Invasion of Barcelona," critically outlines the distress reaped on the city as a result of ever-growing Airbnb tourism (there are close to twenty thousand active Airbnb listings in Barcelona).[138] Airbnb tends to saturate the rental market and drive up rental costs as landlords are able to earn a lot more by renting out their apartment nightly or weekly to Airbnb tourists as opposed to placing it on the regular rental market. This also impacts the overall worth of a property, leading to increased building values, which in turn has a trickle-down effect in the form of gentrification of entire neighborhoods.[139]

In many cities around the world, therefore, the lodging industry as well as resident and tenant associations are lobbying local and federal authorities to enforce stricter regulations around Airbnb.[140] Here we see a strong tension *within* the microculture of the sharing economy around Airbnb, which pits meanings associated with tourism and travel, exchange, convenience, adventure and "authenticity" of experience for its users against meanings such as gentrification and degradation of residential life when considered from the perspective

---

[137] Rebecca Mead, "The Airbnb Invasion of Barcelona," *New Yorker*, April, 29, 2019, https://www.newyorker.com/magazine/2019/04/29/the-airbnb-invasion-of-barcelona; Gerdeman, "The Airbnb Effect."
[138] Mead, "Airbnb Invasion of Barcelona."
[139] Mead, "Airbnb Invasion of Barcelona."
[140] Gerdeman, "The Airbnb Effect."

of residential neighborhoods and urban planning. There are also tensions *between* the (Airbnb) sharing economy microculture and the conventional hotel microculture as each tries to "win" a dominant place in the broader macroculture of lodging and accommodation or tourism.

As mentioned, the broader social context around Airbnb is the sharing economy. While the sharing economy is often presented as espousing environmental, local and community values, it is also driven by practices of commercialization, which prioritize the capitalist structure of private ownership—e.g., of bikes, cars, offices, accommodations—since all of these spaces or objects are ultimately owned by a company or an individual who pays a commission to a bigger company (as is the case with Airbnb or Uber). They also rely on markets for their operation.[141] There is thus a strong tension within the sharing economy microculture between the horizontal ethical principles of exchange and sharing it claims to espouse and the highly monetized relationships that (also) clearly define its structure.

However, there is another perspective on how the sharing economy has impacted the broader rental marketplace or tourism industry. Some analysts suggest that corporate culture has in fact *adapted* to the fundamental principles espoused by the sharing economy: "concepts such as connectivity, openness, community and building bridges. Corporations are now recognizing the importance of relationships—and sharing—in how they do business."[142] Some conventional businesses and industries have indeed been forced to make changes in order to remain viable as a result of the influence (and success) of the sharing economy. In the macroculture of lodging and accommodation, major hotel chains like Marriott International have started adding "experience packages" to compete with the growing expanse of services offered by Airbnb.[143] And in the macroculture of car services, the ridesharing microculture has had strong gains over

---

[141] Anitra Nelson, "'To Market, to Market': Eco-collaborative Housing for Sale," in *Small Is Necessary: Shared Living on a Shared Planet* (London: Pluto Press, 2018), 211.

[142] Anastasia Belyh, "An Introduction to Sharing Economy," *Cleverism*, March 5, 2015, https://www.cleverism.com/introduction-to-sharing-economy/.

[143] Gerdeman, "The Airbnb Effect."

the more conventional microculture around taxis, as taxi companies have had to adapt in order to compete with services like Uber and Lyft by offering apps that let riders book a cab without having to hail it on the street or call a dispatcher and make it easier to pay by credit card.[144]

Conclusion

We are discussing the five characteristics of microcultures in detail here for two reasons.

The first, and most obvious, is to operationalize the ideas discussed in this book. Knowing these characteristics will help you home in on the microcultures that make up the marketplaces that matter to your business and even identify the structural makeup of those microcultures. Identifying the kind of structure a microculture exhibits will help you understand it better and empathize more easily with the lead users driving that microculture. For example, if you identify a microculture by recognizing the fact that it has created a whole new set of norms and rituals around an established idea, then you'd also be able to empathize with its lead users' desire for change. In the same way, a microculture that is the result of the birth of a completely new idea would likely be led by consumers who have an innate interest in being a part of something groundbreaking and novel. Here, too, knowing the structure can help us understand the microculture better and integrate it into our innovation processes in a much more organic manner.

The second reason for discussing the characteristics of microcultures in detail is to create a common language, one that can be easily used to communicate opportunity and demand spaces. This common language doesn't just benefit "the doers" in organizations, who can now converse more easily with one another within and outside the boundaries of their teams and business units; it also

---

[144] Brian Martucci, "What Is the Sharing Economy – Example Companies, Definition, Pros & Cons," *Moneycrashers*, no date, accessed July 23, 2019, https://www.moneycrashers.com/sharing-economy/.

helps "the doers" manage up more effectively. That is, it helps them take complex thoughts and ideas and transform them into simple frameworks to make the case (to the C-Suite) for the pursuit of certain innovation or market strategies.

Over time, this kind of common language can have a much more significant and often immeasurable impact on an organization. In many cases, we've seen it completely reorient organizations from the top down, making them take a much more consumer-led approach to innovation. We've also seen this common language result in much greater and more open communication across middle and senior management, which in turn creates a conducive environment for experimentation and success. Most importantly, we've seen a common language break down traditional barriers to success, particularly in scenarios where senior management or the C-Suite ends up rejecting incredibly powerful and rich ideas because they just don't understand the consumer-led lens from which those ideas were generated.

Microcultures are a powerful currency for change. Therefore, understanding their structure and makeup can become a key competitive advantage in your role within an organization and even in your career in innovation and market development.

PART THREE

How Microcultures Allow Us to Rethink Research for the Purpose of Innovation

CHAPTER FIVE

Reducing the Stress around Innovation and Creating a Culture of Discovery

Innovation at any organization is hard. The professionals tasked with driving growth via innovation are essentially tasked with predicting the future. And this burden can over time become both taxing and grueling. But help is on the way. As you will see in the pages to come, this chapter investigates the culture of stress that permeates much of the product development process. We then present the approach of microcultures as a solution to this problem and show how it can be especially effective in large organizations.

In the previous two sections of this book, we concentrated primarily on how microcultures function in the context of consumer decision-making and how these (relatively) small cultures indicate the broader shifts that will transpire in the marketplace. Microcultures today will impact and shape the mainstream tomorrow. Now, we shift our lens to show you how, by embracing and using the microcultures approach, an organization can reduce the strain that can create tension when a team is looking to innovate. To best understand the power of microcultures, we will focus on one of the most challenging stages of the innovation process—the front end or research stage.

We outlined and provided a definition for this stage in Chapter One: it includes discovering opportunities, prioritizing them and then determining the right time to develop them. As part of our conversation about the key stress driver in the innovation process, we'll home in on an aspect of the research stage that is particularly stressful: scoping. Because when businesses rely on defining the exact boundaries of what their research will cover *before* commissioning a research study of the marketplace, a tremendous amount of pressure is placed on *getting things right*. But scoping, as we will discuss, is an inexact science prone to confirmation bias and misleading assumptions. We will show you how, with microcultures and the use of big data tools, we can significantly reduce the stress *and* inaccuracies around the process of research for innovation.

Did we mention that 80 to 95% of innovations fail?

As we explained in Chapter One, the failure rate of innovations hovers somewhere between 80 and 95%.[145] This means that, by definition, innovation is a high-risk field where failures are perceived as inevitable. It is no surprise then that innovation professionals are mired in anxiety and can become prone to overcompensate. One form of overcompensation is conducting *too much* research ("death by data").

This culture of over-research is dominant in innovation departments and large companies and is a typical component of how business professionals cope with the stress of their jobs. They're driven by fear of failure and as a result, they're compelled to do excessive amounts of research to double, triple and quadruple check every single potential idea or approach. Often, what ends up happening is that the right time to enter into the marketplace passes because entry is pushed too far ahead. Suddenly companies find themselves in a mad dash to the finish line, surrounded by three of their closest competitors who

---

[145] Hill, Jones, and Schilling, *Strategic Management Theory*; Dillon, "I Think of My Failures as a Gift"; Schneider and Hall, "Why Most Product Launches Fail"; Blackburn, "Speed to Market."

eventually force them back to the model of competing on price and features (rather than owning an emotional early-mover advantage).

Uncovering the Primary Drivers of Stress

Before we go any further and deconstruct the elements of the research stage of the innovation process to understand the contributors to stress, we need to back up a little and understand the innovation process itself. Doing so gives us the context needed to empathize with innovation departments and understand why they currently do what they do.

These are the two most common types of innovation: *renovation* and *net new product development*.

First, let us talk about innovation that exists in the form of a *renovation*. As the name suggests, it occurs when a company takes an existing product and makes some sort of (seemingly minor) change to it. For example, Kraft might take its Kraft Dinner product and modify it by adding slightly "better" ingredients, as it did in 2007 when it replaced its 100% basic wheat flour noodles with 50% whole grains, or in 2016 when it started using natural spices like paprika and turmeric to give the pasta its iconic orange color instead of using synthetic food coloring, as it had done before. This latter change was brought on as a response to consumers who had started protesting against the health risks associated with Yellow 5 and Yellow 6 food dyes that were being used in traditional Kraft Dinner products.[146] The company reacted to its consumer base by replacing these ingredients with healthier ones, ultimately retaining the same product but with a meaningful modification. This is what we'd call a classic *renovation*.

One might also think back to the intriguing and quite notorious case of Coca-Cola's launch of "New Coke" back in 1985. Reacting to decreasing market shares because of competition from the PepsiCo company, Coke underwent a slight "renovation," becoming slightly

---

[146] Carmen Chai, "Kraft Dinner to Remove Synthetic Colours by 2016, Company Says," *Global News*, April 20, 2015, https://globalnews.ca/news/1949205/kraft-dinner-to-remove-synthetic-colours-by-2016-company-says/.

sweeter while being rebranded by the company as "New Coke." Upon its release, Coca-Cola sales increased by 8%, but then a major backlash came from the American Deep South, where Coca-Cola is considered part of regional identity. People there felt betrayed and even alienated by the new formula, calling and writing to the company's Atlanta headquarters in droves to complain. Psychiatrists were even brought in to deal with these consumers because they were so distraught by the rebranded product and were said to be talking about New Coke as "they would discuss the death of a family member."[147] Within seventy-nine days of bringing New Coke to market, Coca-Cola pulled it from the shelves and brought back the original version but with a new label: "Coca-Cola Classic." By the end of that year, the new old drink was outselling both New Coke and Pepsi Cola.

The story doesn't end there though. In the summer of 2019, thirty-four years later, the Coca-Cola Company has reintroduced New Coke to the market, this time as a limited edition collector's pack and with a rebranding that links it to the hit Netflix series *Stranger Things*, which is set in the year that New Coke was originally introduced. The idea came from the series' creators, Ross and Matt Duffer, who wanted to use the beverage to promote the show. There are several product placements of New Coke scattered throughout the show's third season, which premiered in July 2019.

The second kind of innovation we need to talk about occurs when a company introduces a *net new product*. For example, Coca-Cola may decide to create its own fermented beverage,[148] or a food company

---

[147] Palmer Haasch, "New Coke is the Weirdest Pop Culture Throwback in Stranger Things 3," *Polygon*, July 6, 2019, https://www.polygon.com/2019/7/6/20683542/stranger-things-3-new-coke-1985-coca-cola-where-to-buy; see also Eric Francisco, "New Coke Joke in 'Stranger Things' Dusts off a Soda that Died 17 Years Ago," *Inverse*, July 3, 2019, https://www.inverse.com/article/57348-stranger-things-season-3-new-coke-real-brief-history-controversy-conspiracy. There are several books that were published on the topic, see, e.g., Thomas Oliver, *The Real Coke, The Real Story* (New York: Random House, 1987).

[148] In 2018, the Coca-Cola Company acquired Australian-based kombucha maker Organic & Raw Trading Co., which makes the MOJO brand of naturally fermented kombucha drinks. Coca-Cola has not introduced or developed its own fermented beverage, however. Coca-Cola Company, "Coca-Cola Adds First Line of Kombucha

may decide to introduce a brand new plant-based yogurt (e.g., Danone introduced a new line of plant-based yogurts in early 2019, along with opening the largest vegan yogurt plant in the country).[149] Or, take the groundbreaking case of drop-out engineering student Richard Drew who, by force of luck and persistence, was hired by the 3M Company in 1921 to test a variety of sandpapers at local auto shops. Not a particularly compliant employee, Drew ended up spending the majority of his working hours trying to figure out a problem he had witnessed in many of the auto shops where he was going to distribute the company's sandpaper for testing. At the time, two-tone paint was especially popular on cars. In order to achieve this effect, auto workers had to cover up part of the paint job with adhesive tape while painting. In those years, all that was available for doing this was an especially aggressive kind of tape that would inevitably rip off chips of the fresh paint on cars when it was removed. This made the process incredibly arduous and frustrating for the workers. Drew set about finding a solution using resources from the 3M Company despite a lack of support from his employers. In 1930, he invented Scotch Brand Masking Tape (what we know as masking tape today—a nonaggressive tape that can easily be removed without damaging surfaces) and soon after, he developed the world's first transparent tape, today known ubiquitously as Scotch tape. This being the early 1930s with the advent of the Great Depression, Drew's innovation hit the market with perfect timing. People could no longer afford to buy new things because of the economic strain of the times and so, Scotch tape became the ideal product for repairing broken items that people could no longer afford to replace. The 3M Company ended up thriving during the Depression era, a period when most other businesses were crashing.[150]

---

through Acquisition of Australian-based Organic & Raw Trading Co.," *Coca-Cola Company*, September 19, 2018, https://www.coca-colacompany.com/stories/the-coca-cola-company-adds-its-first-line-of-kombucha-through-ac.

[149] Taylor, Leach, "Danone Unveils Largest Vegan Yogurt Plant in U.S.," *Dairy Herd*, February 13, 2019, https://www.dairyherd.com/article/danone-unveils-largest-vegan-yogurt-plant-us.

[150] Zachary Crockett, "The Man Who Invented Scotch Tape," *Priceonomics*, December 30, 2014, https://priceonomics.com/the-man-who-invented-scotch-tape/.

Nowadays of course, especially within larger organizations, renovational innovations are far more common than net new product launches. Interestingly though, this doesn't make the process of innovation any less stressful or any easier.

To understand why, we need to first make sense of what's at stake once a decision to pursue a new idea has been made. Once the green light has been given to launch a product, companies—especially large organizations—usually invest a lot of resources such as time and money as they figure out details around the new product's logistics, sourcing, manufacturing/line management, distribution, and so on (in Chapter One, this is what we referred to as the second part of the innovation process). For example, if you are a food packaging company and you have developed a formula for a new product or a new version of an existing product, innovation will inevitably involve many changes, like sourcing new ingredients, securing new manufacturers and potentially changing the production line and the logistics around that. It would also involve changes to the packaging to reflect the innovation and maybe also changes in how the product is distributed. Depending on what your food packaging company is launching exactly, the new product may need to get distributed to a new network of retailers or it might require refrigeration where it did not before, and so on.

Interestingly, the steps in this second part of the innovation process are actually fairly standard *once the new idea has been agreed on* and given the green light for production. But they are expensive (in terms of both human and financial capital) and so, all the stress is put on the process of *getting to that green light*, that is, on the steps required in the first part of the innovation process: the research involved in figuring out what is a lucrative idea (and then nurturing it on to the next stage of design and production) or a bad idea (and destroying it early on so as not to squander resources to further develop it at the next stage). In short, many of us may not realize it, but it is actually the research stage during the front half of the innovation process that is the primary driver of stress, rather than the steps taken afterwards.

Of course, there are some leaders that we often think of as having a great instinct for innovation. Such leaders may do little research or may just have an innate ability to rely on their gut to get to the right ideas. Richard Drew, for example, who was described by one of his colleagues as an "oddball," had a brilliant innovation because he had a terrific sense of instinct and didn't care about what his employers wanted from him.[151] We can think of other unconventional paradigm-changing innovators, like Steve Jobs or Nikola Tesla, who had similarly impressive capacities for gut instinct (and disregard for authority) that allowed them to succeed. But none of these are typical cases. Unfortunately, the majority of us cannot rely on instinct (which has been shown to result in error and bias most of the time anyway)[152] or superhuman character traits. As a result, anxiety and stress remain a key element of the innovation process for the majority of us because we rely so heavily on that research process.

Now that we've identified the research process as the culprit, let's unpack why this process is so notoriously difficult. The reality is that it is far from easy to figure out what is a "good" and what is a "bad" idea in terms of product development and innovation. It requires starting with a true process of discovery, ideally a reliable and rigorous process of research and data collection that enables us to accurately identify and prioritize new opportunities or demand spaces[153] and then determine the right time to develop them. In large organizations, however, consumer research is vulnerable to institutional pressures, which traditionally involve an overreliance on scoping. Scoping means starting the whole process by defining the exact boundaries of what the research will cover *before* even commissioning the actual research project and learning anything about consumer needs and pain points. As we often mention in this book, this is primarily driven by the

---

[151] Crockett, "The Man Who Invented Scotch Tape."

[152] John Maule, "How Stress Impacts Decision Making," *Leeds University Business School Blog*, May 2, 2017, https://business.leeds.ac.uk/dir-record/research-blog/712/how-stress-impacts-decision-making.

[153] Demand space is defined as the *intersection* of *the consumer's specific context* (e.g., demographic profile, time of day, where that consumer is and with whom) and *the consumer's emotional and functional needs*. For example, is the consumer a diabetic young woman alone at her work desk craving a 3 p.m. snack? Or is the consumer a teenage boy out with his friends at the local mall to watch a movie on the weekend? And so on.

overreliance on the "industry lens" as a key driver for organizational strategy on the part of its leaders.

So, in order to know what we're going to study, we end up relying on industry reports and gut feeling. Based on these *highly inaccurate metrics*, we then write a research brief with the exact set of questions we would like answered. This requires undue attention to *getting it right* because otherwise, the rest of the research ends up tainted and precious resources like time and money get wasted. This is exactly where the stress begins—right at the top of the process.

The main problem with the process of "scoping" is that research then rarely ends up being a purely exploratory process because there is strong pressure to prove the underlying hypothesis that is driving a particular project (what is known as confirmation bias, discussed below). In such cases, research will invariably move in a predictable direction, and the prospect of finding or recognizing new and powerful insights becomes unlikely, if not altogether impossible. *We call this scope bias* and argue that when we define the boundaries of a project too narrowly and in a pre-set way, our chances for thinking outside the box and thus coming up with innovative ideas are severely compromised.

Companies, however, find it very difficult to avoid scope bias because *they think* that defining the scope of a project will help them stay on budget and on schedule. This mind-set is the result of companies' overreliance on traditional research methodologies (surveys, focus groups, interviews) that are time-sensitive and service-driven: someone (or in most cases, a team) has to design the questionnaire, run the focus groups or interviews, analyze the data, build presentations, do the song and dance with their clients, etc. Such structured data-gathering methods leave research teams with no choice but to *dictate* exactly which areas to gather data from and which areas to avoid. It's the only way for them to keep tabs on what they're doing and how much they're going to spend in the process.

Microcultures to the Rescue

Microcultures can help solve this problem by providing research with agility and eliminating the need to scope. We can start with pretty much nothing and get all the information we need to make decisions. For example, as a clothing manufacturer, we might be interested in launching a new line in women's apparel. So, we would start by analyzing the microcultures surrounding the topic of apparel for women and, by using big data ethnography, we would quickly discover a microculture of size inclusivity and size-inclusive design. We would also learn that this microculture is emerging (growing significantly) and specifically applies to swimwear and urban women between the ages of 35 and 54 (which aligns with our interests).

Based on this information, we could confidently launch a new swimwear brand with these parameters of size inclusivity and size-inclusive design in mind, knowing that this is currently an unmet consumer need in the marketplace. The process of research that microcultures enable is one of "following the breadcrumbs." As researchers, big data and the ethnographic method enable us to follow the clues inadvertently left by the consumer through the (millions of) organic conversations they have on a day-to-day basis across the Internet (and across geographies).

Such an accurate reflection of the marketplace is hard to come by when we scope projects first. As we already alluded to above, one of the major issues with scoping is *confirmation bias*, a type of cognitive bias that involves favoring information that confirms one's previously existing beliefs or biases. Coined by British psychologist Peter Wason, the term refers to how our biases influence how we gather, interpret and recall information. Generally, we fail to notice and will even willfully ignore objective facts and instead interpret information in a way that ultimately reinforces our existing beliefs and assumptions. Clearly, we miss a lot of important information when we do this. Psychologist C. James Goodwin, for example, shows how confirmation bias helps reinforce an individual's belief in extrasensory perception.

> Persons believing in extrasensory perception (ESP)
> will keep close track of instances when they were

"thinking about Mom, and then the phone rang and it was her!" Yet they ignore the far more numerous times when (a) they were thinking about Mom and she didn't call and (b) they weren't thinking about Mom and she did call. They also fail to recognize that if they talk to Mom about every two weeks, their frequency of "thinking about Mom" will increase near the end of the two-week-interval, thereby increasing the frequency of a "hit."[154]

Examples like this are in line with the findings of Wason's rule discovery test, a series of experiments conducted in 1960, which proved that the majority of people do not try to critically test or disprove their hypotheses but rather try to confirm them. Or, to cite a young girl recently interviewed on the hugely popular photoblog/social media feed, *Humans of New York*: "I'm also fascinated by how the human mind deals with death. It's like people shut down the idea of death completely, and insist that heaven and hell are places after death. But death is death. And everyone after death is dead, because consciousness is just your brain. And even if there is evidence of life after death, it's difficult to assess. We're going to be incredibly biased toward any information that suggests there's something more. Because we are so desperate to believe it."[155] In the context of business scoping, this is fatal because it prevents us from noticing what we don't already know, and when we conduct research, we tend to simply confirm rather than try to falsify a hypothesis. Thus, we invariably come right back to the same old idea.

The confirmation bias inherent in scoping is also closely related to what sociologist Erving Goffman calls *frame analysis*, a theory he

---

[154] Cited in Kendra Cherry, "How Confirmation Bias Works," *VeryWell Mind*, last modified September 8, 2019, https://www.verywellmind.com/what-is-a-confirmation-bias-2795024.

[155] Brandon Stanton, "Adults Guess and Assume That I'm Not Going to Understand Things Just Because I'm a Little Kid," *Humans of New York, Facebook*, August 6, 2019, https://www.facebook.com/humansofnewyork/photos/a.102107073196735/3307521479321929/?type=3&theater.

proposed in the early 1970s to explain how people organize their experiences. He argues that human beings engage with the world around them by relying on frameworks (what cognitive psychologists would call a schema—abstract mental structures or models),[156] with which to understand their reality and reduce the complexity of the world. A framework, argues Goffman, "allows its user to locate, perceive, identify, and label a seemingly infinite number of concrete occurrences defined in its terms."[157] Frames are ultimately used as a shortcut of sorts to interpret information—but from a particular vantage point or within the context of a specified set of meanings (increasing the risk of confirmation bias). But all this is part of a two-part process, whereby frames not only help us *interpret* our world but also contribute to our particular *reconstruction* of that world. And, as with much of our experience of social reality—be it the symbolism guiding our communication, the fields that determine our habitus, our rationalizations for making decisions, and so on (see Chapter Two)—we rarely recognize the actual principles (or biases) that guide and define the frames within which we operate.[158] As Goffman writes, people take frames for granted and are "likely to be unaware of such organized features as the framework has and unable to describe the framework with any completeness if asked."[159] Because frames are ultimately shortcuts that people use to organize the vast amount of information in the world, there are inevitably things that fall to the wayside, either as a result of confirmation bias or maybe because of how information is presented to us by another source (e.g., industry performance reports and forecasts).

The implication here is that it's difficult to retain or recognize new information unless it conforms to our established ideas about the

---

[156] Jean Piaget, *The Origins of Intelligence in Children* (New York: International University Press, 1952).

[157] Erving Goffman, *Frame Analysis: An Essay on the Organization of Experience* (New York: Harper & Row, 1974), 21.

[158] William Gamson, "Review of Frame Analysis: An Essay on the Organization of Experience by Erving Goffman," *Contemporary Sociology* 4, no. 6 (1975): 604.

[159] Goffman, *Frame Analysis*, 21.

world.[160] So, rather than looking at the big picture, we only see what we have chosen to zoom in on; everything outside of the frame remains out of view. Framing is implicit in the act of defining the scope of a project. When we set boundaries and write the questions that we would like answered *prior to* conducting any sort of meaningful research about unmet consumer needs or net new revenue opportunities, we construct a rigid frame around our topic, a frame with implicit assumptions and biases about what we expect to "discover."

As mentioned, framing is also about how information gets conveyed to people. A common application of Goffman's theory is in media and mass communication. For example, we might think of how a particular media outlet focuses on one particular event and places it within a specific field of meaning, while another media outlet—one that has a different ideological orientation, for example - might focus on the same event but frame and interpret it differently. Take the early August 2019 mass shootings in El Paso, Texas, for example, which were covered in significantly different ways by Fox News and CNN as well as other, more left-leaning media outlets. Fox News, which is classically the mouthpiece of the right wing and the Republican Party, framed the mass shooting in various ways—as a mental health issue, as a result of influence from violent video games, as part of a broader ISIS conspiracy to send terrorists to the US across the Mexican border— but condemned any attempt to frame the event in the context of gun law restriction or reform, white supremacy and racism or (toxic) masculinity and misogyny (the key frames used by more left-leaning media outlets).[161]

The concept of frame is of utmost importance because it's ultimately

---

[160] See the 2015 *New Yorker* article titled "Why Facts Don't Change Our Minds" for an overview of recent studies in cognitive psychology that explain the human tendency to reject evidence-based knowledge in lieu of deeply ingrained beliefs and assumptions. Elizabeth Kolbert, "Why Facts Don't Change Our Minds," *New Yorker*, February 19, 2017, https://www.newyorker.com/magazine/2017/02/27/why-facts-dont-change-our-minds.

[161] See, e.g., John Whitehouse, "How Fox News Pushed Propaganda about the El Paso Mass Shooting," *Media Matters for America* (MMFA), August 4, 2019, https://www.mediamatters.org/fox-news/how-fox-news-pushed-propaganda-about-el-paso-mass-shooting.

about how information is presented, which invariably influences how people choose to process and interpret that information. In terms of the CNN versus Fox News case, for example, this could have significant implications for people's voting choices in the 2020 US elections. But what does this all mean in the context of consumer behavior and the research that large companies invest in to make sense of that behavior? Let's look at the topic of vegan diets to make this clearer.

If we define the scope of a study as vegan diets and their impact on ready-to-eat snacks, the researcher will seldom bother to expand their data-gathering efforts outside of the snacking universe (or frame). They want to keep time and resources in check, which are at a premium because the methods employed are services-driven and are affected by the number of hours a project ultimately takes to build and complete.

But this can be detrimental to the outcome of the research. What if the cultural universe of vegan diets was more strongly connected to replacing meals rather than consuming snacks? In such a scenario, we'd end up studying a universe that isn't naturally connected to the way consumers use vegan foods in their lives. When we scope in this way, what we are really doing is constructing a rigid frame around our topic with implicit assumptions (often created by the industry we work in) about what we *think* we're going to see. And so the act of scoping in such a situation would ultimately result in missed opportunities—e.g., the cultural universe of meal replacements that sits *outside* of the frame that we have chosen—that could have saved the team from launching a failed product. Or better yet, that could have allowed the team to launch something that would have solved a truly unmet need and taken the market by storm.

If we want to improve the overall accuracy of research and genuinely uncover net new opportunities for our businesses, we need to eliminate the need to scope altogether. Microcultures allows us to do that by giving research agility. And, as outlined in Chapter Three, due to the incredible advances made in AI technology and the availability of big data, we can easily access large samples while also gaining a clear understanding of the particular context(s) in which these samples are situated. More importantly, we can do this in a matter of minutes and hours rather than weeks and months.

Microcultures thus generate a more secure process of trend identification, thereby enabling us to more confidently decide how and when to launch new products. Innovation and R&D professionals can thus avoid the "death by data" syndrome as they will feel less pressure to overtest and overvalidate every single idea before it's brought to life. The application of machine learning in the research process means that we can quickly generate complex analyses of *the entire universe* of nuanced meanings that consumers create (around the topic or area of study) in an ongoing manner through their online conversations. Of course, we get to see the information that lies "outside" of the frame too. When we take such an approach, we in fact *let the consumer lead* the way to the opportunities that exist.

Going back to the example of vegan diets and snacking, the consumer-led approach would push us to begin our research from the highest possible layer of abstraction so we could then work our way down to understand the role of vegan diets in snacking, without compromising our ability to identify opportunities—even if they don't directly prove the underlying hypothesis. For example, we could have uncovered that vegan diets are actually more relevant to nonvegans in the context of dinners and weight loss rather than in the context of snacks. This means that vegan snacks appeal to a smaller market and show little growth potential (compared to vegan solutions for dinner or weight loss).

This is just an example, but the point is that the process of innovation functions in a fundamentally different way when we transform an industry-led perspective on scope into an agile, consumer-led perspective that is no longer vulnerable to a researcher's propensity for confirmation bias or a narrow framing of topics. We can then truly describe the consumer-led approach as a culture of discovery because it is all about agile research techniques that allow new information to be discovered and recognized.

Of course, there are many aspects to bringing an innovation to life beyond the process of identifying opportunities. This is why a lot of pressure is placed on the decision of "what to do" and "when to do it," which is what causes incredible stress early on in the innovation process. It's not the aspects of the product launch or logistics around finding a new distributor that cause stress; rather, knowing the financial implications of what follows after a decision is made drives the stress during the early stages of the innovation process. Hence, as much as the process of discovery is critical to early stage innovation, so is the process of idea refinement.

Refinement here can be thought of as the step in which we take the identified opportunities, distill them down into a small list of those relevant to our business and ongoing strategy and then quantify their value to the business. This, we argue, is the only way to make truly informed decisions. The ability to quantify the value of ideas relative to one another and the ability to see clearly into the future are essential to refining a project. Without them, we only confirm our biases further and reinforce our reliance on a hunch. With only a hunch to guide us, we are afraid we are making a mistake, and so we end up trying to piece together a rationale by looking at what others in the industry are doing, gathering data from multiple disparate sources that don't talk to one another, or simply guessing. All of these approaches point us further in the wrong direction, making us even more desperate, exacerbating our fear that we are making a mistake.

Once again, microcultures can help solve this problem because they give us the ability to size the different microcultures of opportunity that exist within a context (see Chapter Three). Going back to our example of women's apparel, we are able to determine that in addition to the presence of a smaller but growing microculture of size inclusivity, there is also an emerging microculture of gender fluidity around fashion choices. How did we know which microculture to pursue? With the application of big data ethnography, we could see that the inclusivity microculture was larger and growing faster. Big data and modern technologies like AI allow us not only to identify emerging microcultures but also to quantify the relative growth and size of the microcultures that make up a broader trend in the marketplace. *These are the exact kinds of features that enable rather than inhibit innovation.* Let's look at two examples of what clients of ours actually experienced when they replaced traditional scoping techniques with a microcultures-led approach in their innovation research process.

One of our clients makes condiments. The majority of their

condiments is sweetened by high-fructose corn syrup. They were looking to replace this sweetener with a slightly better form of sugar. This decision was driven by an ongoing dip in sales and an increase in data showing that the target consumer (middle-class American families) had moved closer to the health-driven consumer and was increasingly being influenced by diet trends like keto, Whole30, Clean Eating, etc.

Furthermore, through research they had already found that allulose, a low-calorie sweetener that the FDA had recently approved as a sugar replacement, was linked (in the consumer's mind) to the keto diet, which was very popular at the time.[162] And so our client considered exploring a series of keto-friendly sugar substitutes for high-fructose corn syrup. This is the direction that a traditionally scoped research project would have taken: identifying diet-friendly and, in particular, keto-friendly sugar substitutes and examining how they are perceived by the American middle class.

By contrast, with the microcultures framework in hand, we set about studying this marketplace by taking a step back and exploring the microcultures around health and food in general. We wanted to follow the breadcrumbs that the consumer inadvertently leaves for us and that ultimately help us to discover the organic opportunities that offered new revenue potential. Along the way we looked for natural ways in which consumers might be linking a microculture around sugar or sugar ingredients to condiments. We ended up with a few different microcultures as we explored the demand space of healthfulness around food.

The biggest of these microcultures was one around weight loss, but it wasn't showing any signs of growth. It linked to a series of

---

[162] Keto is short for ketogenic and is a diet that involves high fat and low carb intake, which—according to some studies—puts your body into a metabolic state called ketosis. When the body is in ketosis, it allegedly becomes more efficient at burning fat for energy. It has been linked to some weight loss and health benefits, but the scientific community continues to debate its value and warn of significant health risks. See, e.g., Harvard Health Publishing, "Should You Try the Keto Diet?" *Harvard Health Website*, October 2018, https://www.health.harvard.edu/staying-healthy/should-you-try-the-keto-diet.

diets like keto (most dominant), Whole30, Clean Eating and paleo, among others. The second microculture was about wellness and overall healthy living. In particular, the notion of wellness focused on reducing mental cloudiness by eating better. It stressed lowering one's carbohydrate intake and increasing one's healthy fats intake. The wellness microculture also linked heavily to fermentation and the introduction of fermented foods into one's diet in order to further enhance cognitive abilities. The third microculture had to do with sugar intake, specifically the desire to learn about and incorporate ways to consume sugars that are low in glycemic value (lower on the index). Of course, allulose was a part of this narrative but so were erythritol, maltitol and other sugars.

Through big data ethnography, we discovered that it's not a specific ingredient like allulose that will provide the competitive advantage but rather a type of sugar—one that is low on the glycemic index. Furthermore, we also discovered that the perfect marriage between sugar and fermentation could create the ideal wellness-related competitive advantage in the condiments marketplace. Now *this* was an interesting and powerful insight, because it did multiple jobs simultaneously: it wasn't just about people who wanted to follow the keto diet specifically, but it was also about people who wanted to benefit from certain keto-friendly (or diet-friendly) ingredients in their day-to-day diet. This meant that the target consumers would not exclusively be people following keto—or any other such diet for that matter—but rather people who introduced certain elements of keto in order to draw on some of the diet's health benefits. The focus of this opportunity space (or demand space), which was growing and emerging, was really on sugar and fermentation and on how the two naturally work well together to create various health benefits for consumers.

This allowed the client to identify a microculture that was large enough to impact their business and that grew fast enough for them to believe in its long-term potential.

This is an important example because we can see how, if our client would have used typical research methods involving scoping, it is inevitable that they would have constructed a frame around their topic that would have blocked the view of unexpected information, such as the growing interest in the combination of sugar and fermentation. Moreover, it would have taken them approximately six months of ongoing research to arrive at a/this series of superficial findings. But by using big data ethnography, they were instead able to arrive at the rich results mentioned above in three days and could then go into the field to validate and design around some of these insights by creating prototypes and running various types of tests. Our client found the results to be phenomenal, so they took the line to market. The entire process was condensed into six months as opposed to eighteen (the typical amount of time spent by innovation and R&D departments on a project from start to finish), which in turn also reduced the anxieties and stress levels associated with making a major innovation decision like this.

Another client of ours was interested in expanding their line of baby products but was unsure about the demand spaces currently worth exploring in that market. They had a sense that organic baby clothing might be a hot item and they had recognized a strong relationship with issues like breastfeeding versus formula feeding from a focus group they had run with first-time mothers. They hired a consultant to design a series of surveys for them to probe deeper into these potential demand spaces. The results did not provide much new information, however, and they remained unsure of the direction in which they should take their existing line of baby products. They sensed that the market needed something new but they were worried about whether it would be worth the effort and money to invest in a new product line—especially since they didn't know exactly what that should entail. That's when they came to us for consultation. They asked us to explore the demand spaces in the context of baby products as a whole and to look for opportunities that might indicate room for a new branded offering in the space. In a mere three days of research and analysis, our team uncovered a series of interconnected microcultures in the context of baby products that offered incredible opportunity for our client.

First, we found three intersecting microcultures around health, feeding and clothing. In each of these microcultures, it was clear that mothers (the dominant consumer in the baby product market) were concerned with sustainable and eco-friendly products because they felt that what was dangerous for the environment could equally pose a threat to the well-being of their family—an underlying value that was absolutely central to their purchasing decisions. Our analysis not only confirmed this opportunity for the client but also provided them with an estimate of market size and growth potential for this opportunity. This was critical, as it helped the client to not only determine the viability of the idea but also make clear decisions around timing (based on how much and how quickly the microculture was growing). Additionally, what our client's earlier research had failed to notice was the extent to which baby products also sit in a microculture of convenience. While mothers seek to avoid harsh chemicals in products that come into contact with their baby's skin or digestive system, for example, they are also very much driven by a desire for convenient and easy-to-use solutions for feeding and clothing their babies. This is a fact that many mothers who had participated in the initial focus group had been too embarrassed to state explicitly because of the cultural pressures that force them to appear like they're always making maximum effort and not resorting to any shortcuts. We found, for example, that biodegradable packaging had a particularly large core market and growth, especially when compared to its recyclable alternatives. Why? Because biodegradable sits at the intersection of consumers' desire for convenience *and* sustainability. It gives mothers in particular the alibi they need in order to justify the use of "convenient" solutions because it, more importantly, also arms the consumer with much-needed forms of symbolic capital that revolve around sustainable and responsible living.

With this concrete information, our client was able to quickly prototype and test new products like "biodegradable" diapers and cleaning wipes. Once again, a stress-laden process that could have taken over a year and a half to navigate was reduced to just a couple of months, as our client was able to confidently bring a new line to market, knowing in advance what consumers were really looking for and why.

But Why Does Stress Really Matter?

We all know that in small doses, stress can actually have a positive effect, pushing us to work harder, faster and altogether more productively. Numerous scientific studies have proven this, showing how stress produces adrenaline and cortisol hormones in the blood that actually push us to take action, triggering the "fight" component of the "fight or flight" response.[163] But of course there is a flipside to this: the "flight" reaction. There is also a consensus in the scientific community that stress has a breaking point beyond which productivity no longer increases but begins to decrease, as workers become fatigued, distracted, overwhelmed and uninspired to come up with or implement new ideas and even miss more work as a result.[164] In fact, the American Institute of Stress estimates that "job stress costs US industry more than $300 billion a year in absenteeism, turnover, diminished productivity, and medical, legal and insurance costs."[165] There are other implications as well. Heightened levels of anxiety at work can also lead people to fixate on potential threats, which then result in them missing out on big opportunities, as per a study cited in the *Harvard Business Review* on how anxiety affects how CEOs make business decisions.[166] A team of MIT neuroscientists found another negative work-related effect of stress, proving that chronic stress skews decisions toward higher-risk options, especially in

---

[163] Maule, "How Stress Impacts Decision Making." See also Mike Mannor et al., "How Anxiety Affects CEO Decision Making," *Harvard Business Review*, July 19, 2016, https://hbr.org/2016/07/how-anxiety-affects-ceo-decision-making."; Jean MacFadyen, "The Dance Between Innovation, Stress, and Productivity," *Holistic Nursing Practice* 29 (2015): 187–189; Robin Cowan et al., "Productivity Effects of Innovation, Stress and Social Relations," *Journal of Economic Behavior & Organization* 79 (2011): 165–182; Hans Selye, *The Stress of Life* (New York: McGraw-Hill, 1956).

[164] Cowan et al., "Productivity Effects of Innovation, Stress and Social Relations"; MacFadyen, "The Dance Between Innovation, Stress, and Productivity."

[165] American Psychological Association, "Work Stress," *American Psychological Association*, no date, http://www.apaexcellence.org/resources/special-topics/work-stress.

[166] Mannor et al., "How Anxiety Affects CEO Decision Making.".

decision-making that involves cost-benefit conflict.[167] These findings explain how high levels of stress can also play a part in increasing substance abuse and mental health disorders. Furthermore, stress can reduce our ability to think effectively, push us to prematurely home in on a "solution" so as to make the stress go away and increase our reliance on intuitive thinking, which is itself highly correlated with error and bias.[168]

Now that we have a sense of exactly how detrimental stress and anxiety are to productivity, sound decision-making and health in the workplace, let's see how these effects are even more pronounced in the context of innovation—which reflects a quite particular case of work-related stress.

A vast body of research in psychology shows that because innovation involves change, transformation, disruption and thus uncertainty, stress and innovation are inevitable bedfellows. More specifically, researchers have found that "blindly pursuing higher innovation rates may eventually back-fire: the increased amount of change that workers have to deal with will eventually reduce their productivity, and so defeat the purpose of the innovation. In addition, stress spills over to other actors and has a negative effect on social relations [between coworkers], which in turn can lead to yet more stress."[169] Additionally, because of the novelty implied by innovation, a natural outcome of the innovation process is a shift in one's routines. Routines standardize human/coworker interactions and bring predictability and implicit agreement on how to act. Studies have shown that once routines are compromised, cooperation between workers tends to decrease and efficiency is also reduced as a result.[170]

Moreover, because innovation is itself rather vague and difficult to define and measure, the process can seem endlessly demanding and is

[167] Anne Trafton, "Stress Can Lead to Risky Decisions," *MIT News*, November 16, 2017, http://news.mit.edu/2017/stress-can-lead-to-risky-decisions-1116.

[168] Maule, "How Stress Impacts Decision Making."

[169] Cowan et al., "Productivity Effects of Innovation, Stress and Social Relations."

[170] Cowan et al., "Productivity Effects of Innovation, Stress and Social Relations."

thus rendered particularly stressful for those submerged in it.[171] This is yet another major challenge of innovation.

Finally, those same hormones mentioned above—the "fight" hormones that push us to excel—can also cause shortness of breath, a pounding heart, tense muscles and high blood pressure[172]—hardly the optimal physical state in which to be productive, let alone enable the creativity and alertness—the "positive cognitive-affective state of mind"[173]—required to innovate. A major challenge for large organizations is then "knowing how to ensure their capacity for development isn't killed by 'innovation stress'"[174] or, worse yet, burnout, which has not surprisingly been shown to inhibit innovation (among other things).[175]

Conclusion

If we can leverage microcultures effectively, we can significantly impact workers' stress levels. As mentioned, job stress comes with a huge price tag for the US industry due to worker absenteeism, reduced productivity and outrageous medical, legal and insurance bills.[176] As we have shown in this chapter, a microculture approach during the first stage of research in the innovation process takes away most of the debilitating stress involved in bringing new or modified products to market.

Of course, reducing stress is not just about productivity and the success of innovation projects. There is an important emotional and

---

[171] Alf Rehn, "Top 5 Ways to Tackle Innovation Stress in the Workplace," *European CEO*, April 17, 2019, https://www.europeanceo.com/business-and-management/top-5-ways-to-tackle-innovation-stress-in-the-workplace/.

[172] Jessica Day, "The Impact of Stress on Innovation," *Ideascale*, July 10, 2018, https://ideascale.com/impact-of-stress-on-innovation/.

[173] Hannele Huhtala, and Marjo-Riitta Parzefall, "A Review of Employee Well-Being and Innovativeness: An Opportunity for a Mutual Benefit," *Creativity and Innovation Management* 16 (2007), 300.

[174] Rehn, "Top 5 Ways to Tackle Innovation Stress in the Workplace."

[175] Huhtala and Parzefall, "A Review of Employee Well-Being and Innovativeness: An Opportunity for a Mutual Benefit," 304.

[176] American Psychological Association, "Work Stress."

moral dimension to consider as well, namely worker satisfaction. By changing the way research is conducted in large organizations, people will be able to enjoy their jobs more and be more excited about their work, instead of being overrun by anxiety and fear. Microcultures enable organizations to create a true culture of innovation because their employees will be less stressed out and therefore in the optimal frame of mind for making better, more creative and faster decisions.

CHAPTER SIX

Beyond Demographic and Generational Thinking: Why Microcultures Are More Powerful than Segmented Models

In 2005, just a few months before he would take his own life, literary cult hero David Foster Wallace addressed the graduating class at Kenyon College in what is now considered one of the most famous commencement speeches of all time. He began his talk with a parable to describe how the most obvious and important realities of life are often the hardest to see or describe:

> There are these two young fish swimming along, and they happen to meet an older fish swimming the other way, who nods at them and says, "Morning, boys. How's the water?" And the two young fish swim on for a

bit, and then eventually one of them looks over at the other and goes, "What the hell is water?"[177]

In addressing an audience of freshly minted university graduates, Foster Wallace was talking specifically about the trials of adult working life, and urged his young listeners to consider "simple awareness" as a survival method: awareness of what is so real and essential, so hidden in plain sight all around us all the time, that we have to keep reminding ourselves over and over:

"This is water."

"This is water."

"This is water."

Foster Wallace acknowledges how difficult this is. His commencement speech is a challenge "to stay conscious and alive in the adult world day in and day out"[178] and to dedicate ourselves to constantly looking at the world around us in order to assess where we are and what we should choose to do. This is the value of education, he says. It is not about knowledge. It is about embracing awareness. Water is a metaphor for unconsciousness and for how, when you are so deeply immersed in something, you rarely question it—like a fish who is forever swimming through water but unaware that its surroundings are water; like an adult in the rat race who doesn't realize that he is part of the rat race but goes through the agonizing motions anyway. Or, like a researcher who is unaware of the frame through which they have been programmed and conditioned to view their subjects. As a result, they fail to discover rich insights because their field of vision has been reduced by adhering to the status quo.

Our discussion on frames and the limitations of observing the world through them that we started in the previous chapter continues here. In this chapter, we focus on the problem of demographics-driven

---

[177] For the full written and audio transcript of the speech, see Farnam Street, "This Is Water by David Foster Wallace (Full Transcript and Audio)," *Farnam Street*, April 2012, https://fs.blog/2012/04/david-foster-wallace-this-is-water/.

[178] Farnam Street, "This Is Water." See also Jenna Krajeski, "This is Water," *New Yorker*, September 19, 2008, A Review of Employee Well-Being and Innovativeness: An Opportunity for a Mutual Benefit."

research in the context of the innovation process. As explained, human beings use frames as a mental shortcut for making sense of the vast amounts of information in the world. One of the inevitable outcomes of this is that while some information is prioritized (placed *in* the frame of observation), the rest gets overlooked or ignored (pushed *outside of* the frame). In Chapter Five, we explained how this aspect of framing is closely connected to scoping, a common practice in the first phase of the innovation process that determines the exact parameters of the research and the questions that need to be asked—steps that are based on inevitably biased and implicit assumptions (in addition to causing undue stress and anxiety in business professionals). We outlined a more agile and iterative approach to consumer research through the use of microcultures.

In this chapter, we take another standard procedure in the innovation process to task. While it may be difficult to hear, it pays to listen if you are genuinely motivated to beat the 80–95% failure rate of innovation: One of the biggest and most problematic consequences of framing in the research industry is its reliance on demographics-based research and the segmented models that result from it. We will show you how this practice of relying on demographics in order to evaluate opportunities—a standardized practice of consumer research— is far too structural and ends up ignoring the more dynamic and complex shifts taking place in the market as a whole. This approach, for example, ignores the complexity and specificity of *individual* human behavior, since it is guided by the sweeping brush stroke of quantitative measures that segment consumers according to specific group-based variables like socioeconomic status (SES), age, gender or generational location. Like in the David Foster Wallace fish-in-water parable, framing our research around a narrow set of variables causes us to become so immersed in that specific (and narrow) field of vision that we neither recognize the extent to which we are immersed in it nor the rich complexity that exists beyond it.

In contrast, as we will show, the microcultures approach to consumer research does away with the frame entirely, and in doing so immediately expands our view to encompass the *entire* universe of meaning around a subject. As discussed in Chapter

Three, a microcultures-driven research approach (based on big data ethnography) enables us to identify the full range of meanings that consumers create around a topic or issue through broad contextual, machine-led analysis. The microcultures approach is thus immensely more predictive and capable of capturing the nuances of human behavior than the more traditional, demographics-based model (and, as we'll explain later, it also excels at interpreting *why* people believe in the things they do without needing to interview them or make them answer a dreaded twenty-minute survey).

The Shortcomings of Demographics-Based Research and Segmentation

The most common demographic categories that researchers typically focus on are SES, age, gender, ethnicity/race, education, marital status, religion and geographic location. Generation is another especially popular demographic subcategory in consumer research (e.g., baby boomers versus millennials), which we will focus on in more detail below. Consumer research relies on demographics because it is intuitive and straightforward. It offers the promise of helping you discern your target audience and classifies a broad market of consumers into manageable groups based on a set of shared characteristics. It is *the* benchmark of consumer research and marketing: Companies believe that the utilization of such a standardized lens is key in identifying and evaluating opportunities, understanding what customers really want or need and finding the core market for a particular product or service. Demographic variables are also popular for assessing and segmenting consumer behavior into target audiences because they are easily and accurately collected for the entire population by the government, are usually accessible for free as a result (e.g., the US Census, the US Bureau of Labor Statistics) and can be used to extrapolate study findings across the population.[179]

Demographic variables and analyses are thus convenient and

---

[179] Jagdish N. Sheth, "Demographics in Consumer Behavior," *Journal of Business Research* 5 (June 1977): 129–38.

simple to understand, have clear parameters and give us the impression that we are efficiently and "logically" measuring the dimensions and dynamics of consumer populations.

Don't be fooled though.

This is an inherently flawed and inaccurate model for the purpose of innovation.

As we discussed in the previous chapter, when you communicate an idea to someone, you inevitably frame your topic by zooming in on one element of your story while pushing the other parts of the story outside of the edges of that frame. This is a process that tends to happen unwillingly or subconsciously and is charged with implicit assumptions. When we frame our research in terms of demographic variables, we are doing the same thing: we zoom in on one particular variable (age, gender, SES, marital status, etc.) as a way of explaining a certain phenomenon or human behavior and we push any other possible variables out of sight (literally and metaphorically). We also end up limiting ourselves to a framework defined by stereotypes: *What do white men typically snack on during the Super Bowl? What are the most popular services that Hispanic women seek at beauty salons? What stores are millennials most likely to enter at the mall? Which children's clothing websites do middle-class mothers visit the most?*

Framing questions in this way—a typical outcome of structuring research around demographic metrics—will result in answers that are unlikely to be reflective of reality as they leave little room for surprise. Human behavior, however, is rarely consistent when seen through the lens of demographics. For example, research shows that 68% of skin- and bodycare influencers in 2015 were *men*. Or, perhaps even more surprising, 40% of all baby product purchasers lived in households *without* children.[180] Research based on demographic variables would be hard-pressed to capture these rather counterintuitive yet highly significant findings.

Another reason that demographics-driven research has become

---

[180] Both findings are from the Mobile Purchasers & Influencers Report. Google / Ipsos MediaCT, Ipsos Online Omnibus, August 2015 (cited in Lisa Gevelber, "Why Consumer Intent Is More Powerful Than Demographics," *Think with Google*, December 2015, https://www.thinkwithgoogle.com/marketing-resources/micro-moments/why-consumer-intent-more-powerful-than-demographics/).

the standard is because it allows for attitudinal segmentation, a common metric used by companies that target customer groups based on a set of shared attitudes they ostensibly hold. Collecting this kind of data typically involves administering a set of questions based on a twenty-minute survey of *opinions* or *attitudes* about some topic. For example, a researcher from a yogurt company may ask a respondent questions about plant-based proteins as a way of gathering information about that person's attitude toward milk, meat, vegan versus vegetarian diets, and so on. The focus is squarely on *what* the respondent feels rather than on *why* they *believe* what they do. Again, this method of research is alluring because it is easy to collect this type of data. It's decidedly easier to get someone to tell you that they believe it's important to switch to a plant-based diet because they are concerned about animal welfare than to outline the specific reasons *why* they believe this to be so.

Socrates, Shakespeare and Freud have all written and theorized about how ignorant we, as human beings, are of ourselves. Or, as psychologist Peter Halligan states, "Everyone knows what belief is until you ask them to define it."[181] Because beliefs begin to form pretty much from the moment we are born—initially based on sensory perception and then reinforced throughout our lives by our cultural context, especially by the people around us—beliefs are, like water to fish, rather difficult for individuals to discern, let alone make sense of.

It has also been found that people's belief systems are rooted in their basic biology. Using brain scanners, for example, neuroscientists have been able to detect differences in brain activity based on an individual's beliefs. Specifically, these experiments showed that the "fear zone" in the brain was activated more often in subjects with conservative rather than liberal political leanings when they were shown a threatening image. Compared to their liberal counterparts, this evidence indicates that conservatives are more likely to perceive danger in the world, which can explain, for example, why they might believe in and support restrictive immigration policies or tougher

---

[181] Cited in *New Scientist*, "Beliefs – Why Do We Have Them and How Did We Get Them?" *New Scientist*, April 25, 2015, https://www.scmp.com/magazines/post-magazine/article/1773296/beliefs-why-do-we-have-them-and-how-did-we-get-them.

punitive measures such as the death penalty.[182] For innovation professionals, then, this suggests that it is a much more onerous task to account for consumers' beliefs than to, say, understand consumer behavior based on more straightforward and measurable metrics such as age or household income—but we stand to gain so much more about consumers' intentions, motivations and needs by working to make sense of what they believe and why.

We are quite familiar with this resistance to research that is based on people's deeply ingrained belief systems (as opposed to focusing on demographics). When our company was first starting out, we were keen to get press coverage and generate enthusiasm for our pioneering software that could access consumer motivations and values online via big data ethnography. But in an industry where the standard measures are life stage, SES or gender, media outlets were hesitant to promote the *beliefs*-driven model on which our company was based. Why? Because it was "too complex" and didn't (and still doesn't) fit the established frame of consumer research. It is much easier and more effective for a newspaper headline to read "Millennials Don't Trust Doctors!" instead of writing something like "Hype Grows Around Superfoods, Detoxes, Himalayan Salt Lamps, and Magic Crystals as the Medical-Industrial Complex Reinforces its Hold on the US Healthcare System."

While this lengthy headline may seem ironic, it's not. It's in fact based on an online ethnography we conducted that indicated a growing microculture around the wellness industry. Armed with the microcultures approach, we were able to understand *why* this was happening: because substantially sized groups of lead consumers believed that the medical system (what they were increasingly calling the medical-industrial complex) is designed to keep people sick, and that in order to rise above it and take back some control, they need to take a proactive approach in living their lives differently. To achieve this, they readily make sacrifices in food choice and lifestyle and keep close tabs on the latest developments in the wellness industry, which

---

[182] Krueger, cited in *New Scientist*, "Beliefs"; see also Jonas T. Kaplan, Sarah I. Gimbel, and Sam Harris, "Neural Correlates of Maintaining One's Political Beliefs in the Face of Counterevidence," *Scientific Reports* 6 (2016): 39589.

they believe is more conducive to living a healthy life. This group of lead consumers thus regularly makes and buys the "right" kinds of superfoods or other products to keep themselves feeling healthy and in control of their own well-being.

As mentioned above, research based on *generational demographics* is especially alluring to companies (and the media, in popular culture, in everyday language, etc.). Let's turn to this now to round out our discussion of the research industry's reliance on demographics and segmentation and the challenges with doing so.

It is perhaps not a coincidence that what popularized the concept of *generation* was an essay titled, "The *Problem* of Generations," written by German sociologist Karl Mannheim in 1923. Defined as a group of people clustered together based on a shared historical time period, the problem that Mannheim was referring to was the fallacious "attempt to explain the whole dynamic of history from this one factor."[183] This is another way of saying that we reduce the confusing diversity and complexity of social life by focusing on a vague generalization based on someone's birth year.

The concept of generations is a modern invention, first touched on by nineteenth-century European intellectuals and then coined and refined as a term by Mannheim and others in the first part of the twentieth century. During this period, it became popular as a way of distinguishing between the younger and older generation and was used to make sense of the power struggle between these two groups. The category of generations was also meant to offer people a framework for capturing the major societal changes taking place at the time and their impact on different groupings—or generations—of people.

Ironically, despite Mannheim's attempt to call attention to the fundamental flaws of generational thinking, the framework of generations has become *the* standard way of evaluating human behavior and trends today. It is especially appealing to positivist researchers because it is packaged as a "framework of human destiny

---

[183] Mannheim, Karl, "The Problem of Generations" in *Karl Mannheim: Essays*, edited by Paul Kecskemeti (London: Routledge, 1952).

in comprehensible, even measurable form."[184] This might be another way of saying that the category of generations is loved because it's straightforward and quantifiable (or at least appears to be so), *not* because it's accurate or scientifically proven.

The media in particular has jumped on the generational bandwagon in leaps and bounds. It only takes a quick scroll through headlines or online clickbait to see titles such as "3 Unexpected Reasons Baby Boomers are Turning to YouTube,"[185] "You Know You're a Millennial If" or "22 Things only Gen Xers Will Remember."[186] And while you may have never heard of the Xennial generation, it is in fact a thing too, likely invented by or in the media to describe a microgeneration of people born in between Gen X and millennials, roughly 1977–1983. The *New York Times* has talked about it, including with a quiz to help you determine if you're not in fact "secretly a millennial."[187] And numerous other online lists and quizzes abound to help you figure out if you belong to this generation of "straddlers": "20 Signs You're a Xennial Working Mom," "60 Things You'll Only Understand if You Are a Xennial," and "11 Signs That You're a Xennial, Not a Millennial."[188]

---

[184] Mannheim, "The Problem of Generations," 276. *Positivism* is best defined as an approach in the philosophy of science that relies exclusively on *observable* phenomena, that is, things which are measurable and quantifiable, and is opposed to metaphysical speculation. For the study of physics or biology or other natural sciences, such an approach is common sense and will rarely raise eyebrows. When it comes to explanations of a more social, philosophical or psychological nature, however, positivism does not measure up as it fails to consider the significant effect of individual agency, motivations, intent, etc.

[185] Gevelber, "Why Consumer Intent Is More Powerful Than Demographics."

[186] Philip Bump, "Your Generational Identity Is a Lie," *Washington Post*, April 1, 2015, https://www.washingtonpost.com/news/the-fix/wp/2015/04/01/your-generational-identity-is-a-lie/.

[187] Erin McCann and Anya Strzemien, "Are You Secretly a Millennial?" *New York Times*, May 14, 2019, https://www.nytimes.com/interactive/2019/05/14/style/are-you-a-millennial.html.

[188] See Shana Lebowitz and Allana Akhtar, "There's a Term for People Born in the Early '80s who Don't Feel Like a Millennial or a Gen Xer," *Business Insider*, August 22, 2019, https://www.businessinsider.com/xennials-born-between-millennials-and-gen-x-2017-11; Meghann Foye, "20 Signs You Are a Xennial Working Mom," *Working Mother*, April 2, 2018, https://www.workingmother.

Even the authoritative Pew Research Center has caved to this reductive way of thinking, as it pumps out studies with titles such as "Gen Z, Millennials and Gen X Outvoted Older Generations in 2018 Midterms," "Millennial Life: How Young Adulthood Today Compares with Prior Generations," "Black Millennials Are More Religious Than Other Millennials," and so on and so forth.[189]

The problem of generational thinking is that it removes the possibility that individuals are capable of acting beyond the parameters or constraints of their generational location—which in and of itself is a rather arbitrary demarcation (who or what determines when a generation begins and ends?). It assumes that all people born around roughly the same time are exposed to, shaped and influenced by the same historical events in the same way. It is also a perspective brimming with reductive bias and stereotypes, often using the white middle class as its unspoken reference point. Take into consideration these critical examples provided by journalist Rebecca Onion:

> Palmer H Muntz, then the director of admissions of Lincoln Christian University in Illinois, noticed that plenty of kids he encountered on visits to less-privileged schools weren't intensely worried about grades or planning, like the stereotypical millennial. Fred A

---

com/20-signs-you-are-xennial-working-mom; Brian Galindo, "60 Things You'll Only Understand if You Are a Xennial," *Buzzfeed*, March 9, 2018, https://www.buzzfeed.com/briangalindo/things-only-people-born-between-1975-1985-will-truly-get; Notable Life, "11 Signs That You're a Xennial, Not a Millennial," *Notable Life*, June 30, 2017, https://Notablelife.Com/Xennial-Millennial-Definition/.

[189] Anthony Cilluffo and Richard Fry, "Gen Z, Millennials and Gen X Outvoted Older Generations in 2018 Midterms," *Pew Research Center*, May 29, 2019, https://www.pewresearch.org/fact-tank/2019/05/29/gen-z-millennials-and-gen-x-outvoted-older-generations-in-2018-midterms/; Kristen Bialik and Richard Fry, "Millennial Life: How Young Adulthood Today Compares with Prior Generations," *Pew Research Center*, February 14, 2019, https://www.pewsocialtrends.org/essay/millennial-life-how-young-adulthood-today-compares-with-prior-generations/; Jeff Diamant and Besheer Mohamed, "Black Millennials Are More Religious Than Other Millennials," *Pew Research Center*, July 20, 2018, https://www.pewresearch.org/fact-tank/2018/07/20/black-millennials-are-more-religious-than-other-millennials/.

Bonner II, now at Prairie View A & M University in Texas, pointed out that many of the supposed "personality traits" of coddled and pressured millennials were unrecognisable to his black or Hispanic students, or those who grew up with less money. Siva Vaidhyanathan, a cultural historian and media scholar at the University of Virginia, told Hoover: "Generational thinking is just a benign form of bigotry."[190]

When we rely on sweeping generalizations of a group of people based on one isolated variable (such as year of birth), there are other, very significant pieces of information that get left out of the picture. Millennials, for example, are often depicted as technologically savvy but lazy and self-indulgent (e.g., the "me generation," the "selfie generation").[191] But evidence-based research shows a different picture and dispels these common myths: 47% of millennials in management positions have begun working more hours compared with only 38% of Generation X and 28% of baby boomers, more than half of millennials are willing to work long hours and weekends to achieve career success, and one-third of millennials reported working every day of their vacations.[192]

Generational stereotypes also push today's particularly dire economic conditions out of the frame. Author Malcolm Harris explains that, as a result, we ignore significant contemporary factors such as

---

[190] Rebecca Onion, "Against Generations," *AEON*, May 19, 2015, https://aeon.co/essays/generational-labels-are-lazy-useless-and-just-plain-wrong.

[191] E.g., *Time* magazine's cover story from May 20, 2013 by Joel Stein was titled "The Me Me Me Generation: Millennials Are Lazy, Entitled Narcissists Who Still Live with Their Parents," *Time*, May 20, 2013, https://time.com/247/millennials-the-me-me-me-generation/.

[192] Findings cited in Caroline Beaton, "6 Millennial Myths That Need to Finally Die," *Forbes*, September 6, 2016, https://www.forbes.com/sites/carolinebeaton/2016/09/06/6-millennial-myths-that-need-to-finally-die/#2c1453684fa0; See also Richie Norton, "The 14 Most Destructive Millennial Myths Debunked by Data," *Medium*, January 19, 2017, https://medium.com/the-mission/the-14-most-destructive-millennial-myths-debunked-by-data-aa00838eecd6.

unemployment, overpolicing, lack of economic opportunity, tuition increases and mountainous student debt.[193] We think that *Washington Post* correspondent Philip Bump says it best when he writes that, "We obsess over our generations the way we obsess over our horoscopes, recognizing that it's a dumb approximation of who we are but mining every description for the details that we think are correct."[194]

Or, perhaps what we need is simply to look at some basic evidence, as explained in a *Harvard Business Review* article:

> Most of the evidence for generational differences in preferences and values suggests that differences between these groups are quite small. In fact, there is a considerable variety of preferences and values *within* any of these groups. For example, a thorough analysis of 20 different studies with nearly 20,000 people revealed small and inconsistent differences in job attitudes when comparing generational groups. It found that, although individual people may experience changes in their needs, interests, preferences, and strengths over the course of their careers, sweeping group differences depending on age or generation alone don't seem to be supported.[195]

Much like the other demographic variables discussed above, the generational frame is an unreliable way of evaluating consumer behavior and net new revenue opportunities. Researchers are drawn to these categories and methods of evaluating consumer behavior because they are easy: they tell you to simply shift your target audience rather than make any meaningful changes to the product or service

---

[193] Cited in Onion, "Against Generations."

[194] Bump, "Your Generational Identity Is a Lie."

[195] Eden King et al., "Generational Differences at Work Are Small. Thinking They're Big Affects our Behavior," *Harvard Business Review*, August 1, 2019, https://hbr.org/2019/08/generational-differences-at-work-are-small-thinking-theyre-big-affects-our-behavior. See also David Costanza et al., "Generational Differences in Work-Related Attitudes: A Meta-analysis," *Journal of Business Psychology* 27, no. 4 (December 2012): 375–94.

in question. The microculture lens, by contrast, tells you how you might have to change a product based on an evaluation of the changes taking place in culture (either within a microculture) or more broadly (affecting the macroculture). This is obviously a more difficult process to engage in but it is ultimately a more effective one.

As journalist Rebecca Onion argues, "Big, sweeping explanations of social change sell. Little, careful studies of same-age cohorts, hemmed in on all sides by rich specificity, do not."[196] As we have learned from the microcultures approach, trends don't occur in isolation but are continuously feeding off of each other and influencing each other's strength, direction and meaning to consumers at large. Along the same line of thinking, it would be ridiculous to broadly apply trends or phenomena to a whole generation, as if it were a discrete category that was not influenced by anything else.

A Tangible Method of Evaluation: Belief Systems and Symbolic Capital

Despite the flaws caused by our need to simplify and organize how we categorize consumers, we empathize with the complexity that comes with alternative approaches. We need something tangible that can be understood by a variety of different stakeholders in an organization. But we need something more nuanced and accurate as we look to innovate. We thus propose a method of evaluation.

A method that is based on which form of symbolic capital is winning the power game in culture, rather than looking at which demographic group is growing in size or has more money to spend.

Let's place this in the context of a tangible example. Back in Chapter One, we spoke at length of the Fair Oaks Farm scandal, where we identified a relatively small microculture around animal welfare that suddenly started to grow. With the release of a viral video of cows and calves being severely mistreated at Fairlife Milk's

---

[196] Onion, "Against Generations."

flagship dairy farm, the microculture swelled and grew in dominance, systematically beginning to change the context of the broader milk and dairy industry.

In this scenario, as business professionals in the dairy industry we would make subsequent decisions based on the emerging microculture around animal welfare and the impact on the macroculture of dairy it forecast. The segmentation model, by contrast, would say something that actually sounds kind of similar: the attitudes of millennials (generational segmentation) have changed in the direction of animal welfare that leads them to want to reject dairy milk.

The difference may not seem obvious, but it is an important one nevertheless. In the microcultures model, what we're saying is that we'd be making our next business move based on an emerging form of symbolic capital (exhibiting concern for animal welfare) that's clearly winning the power game in the dairy macroculture in this moment in time. While it was previously relevant to only a small group of people, it has now catapulted to phenomenal growth and has become relevant to almost as many people as health/tolerability was just a few months ago. So, now we believe we're seeing two (competing) branches of opportunity around dairy: health/tolerability on the one hand and animal welfare on the other. We may then note that this microculture around animal welfare now skews toward younger consumers between the ages of 25 and 34, although older consumers still make up substantial portions of it.

This version is harder to communicate, harder to grasp and less alluring as a result. It doesn't make a simplified argument about millennials but instead shows the demographic makeup of a culture that is growing and therefore increasingly attracting people from different walks of life. The challenge is that as human beings, we often claim to want rational and logical arguments, even if in reality we tend to make decisions and lead our lives in highly irrational and emotionally driven ways.

But don't take our word for it; listen to what Nobel laureate (in Economic Sciences) and psychology professor Daniel Kahneman has to say about how people make decisions—and why we tend toward the irrational and the emotional more often than not. Kahneman explains cognitive bias (and confirmation bias, and the framing effect, etc.) by describing a dual-system model of the brain, which involves what he calls System 1 and System 2. In the former—the "intuitive" system—we make rapid, automatic, effortless and instinctive choices that are largely driven by emotion and/or habit and that are thus difficult to change or influence. System 1 is also sensitive to subtle environmental cues or signs of danger. By contrast, in System 2— the system of "reasoning"—we are slower, rule-governed, logical, deliberate and effortful.

Kahneman explains how sometimes, System 2 will intervene because it "knows" that System 1 is prone to error or because there is enough time to slowly deliberate. But more often than not, System 2 fails to correct System 1 and so we act quickly, irrationally and intuitively (which sometimes does take us right where we need to be). System 1 is also, by the way, where we store our beliefs. Kahneman argued that although human beings actually have a "very rational system available ... it isn't always engaged."[197] For better or worse, we are driven by our intuitive system much more frequently than our rational one.

These ideas are also linked to Kahneman's concept of What You See Is All There Is (WYSIATI), which describes how people typically fail to take complexity into account, making judgments and reaching decisions based on what they *think* they know and information already available to them—no matter how perfunctory (or biased or inaccurate) that information may be. Think of how quickly you make a judgment about a person when you first meet them. Within seconds and based on a minimal amount of superficial information—facial expression, outfit, posture—you have a sense of whether this person might be a potential friend, lover or someone maybe not worth getting to know at all. Or, think of the ever-growing anti-vaxxer movement,

---

[197] Interview with Daniel Kahneman. Lance Workman, "Daniel Kahneman on the Definition of Rationality and the Difference Between Information and Insight," *The Psychologist* 22 (January 2009): 36–37, http://thepsychologist.bps.org.uk/volume-22/edition-1/most-important-living-psychologist. These ideas originate in Kahneman's award-winning book, *Thinking, Fast and Slow* (2011).

made up of people convinced that vaccines cause autism, even though there's resounding evidence against this.

A 2017 *New Yorker* article aptly titled "Why Facts Don't Change Our Minds" provides a thorough overview, going back to the 1970s, of the many studies that affirm people's natural tendency toward irrationality. This tendency also explains our proclivity for confirmation bias. Cognitive psychologists Hugo Mercier and Dan Sperber argue that the persistence of confirmation bias in human thought and behavior is a sign of its adaptive function; they argue that it reflects our "hypersociability." The ability to reason is a trait humans have developed over time as a means of navigating our predominantly social world (e.g., how to collaborate with others in order to survive) and *not* in order to solve abstract, logical problems or even help us draw conclusions from unfamiliar data. This explains the high preponderance of irrational thinking and confirmation bias. Numerous cognitive psychology books continue to corroborate the extent to which we are in fact irrational animals, with titles like *The Enigma of Reason*, *The Knowledge Illusion* and *Denying to the Grave*.[198]

But we bring up these arguments from cognitive psychology not simply to explain why demographics-based thinking is easier for researchers and business professionals to swallow but also to further prove the extent to which consumers are beliefs-driven, intuitive creatures. People rarely make choices based on logical and thought-out reason, as much as we like to think that we do. Instead, we are emotional, irrational and heavily influenced by our beliefs—a subjective system of "knowledge" that guides each of us in unique ways. Microcultures seek to tap into exactly this kind of "hidden" information: they pick up on consumers' emotional drivers and their unconscious and unmet needs—the kind of information that demographic or generational thinking is incapable of detecting.

This is can be a tough pill for some of our clients to swallow. Because some our clients want the easy, quick and intuitive answer and are reluctant to make big changes to their product line, even if there is abundant evidence for doing so. As stated in the *Harvard*

---

[198] Kolbert, "Why Facts Don't Change Our Minds."

Business Review, "when you define a market not by who's in it but rather by how the people in it think, marketers have a far more complicated and expensive job. Suddenly, 'female' and 'affluent' are replaced with 'adaptive mind-sets' and 'people who seek authenticity.'"[199]

Thinking back to Chapter Two, where we explained how consumers' striving for symbolic capital is ultimately about establishing one's position in a particular community of like-minded people with shared beliefs and values, let's consider how we would deal with research findings that present us with two fathers of the same age behaving in different ways—a very likely possibility, of course, but one that would typically be obscured by studies based on lumping together all millennial dads or all middle-class dads or all divorced dads, and so on. It is obviously easier to work with a statement such as "millennial dads gravitate toward organic food" than to begin understanding why one thirty-year-old dad is in fact a die-hard organic shopper while another dad of the same age couldn't care less about organic products.

As mentioned, when it comes to deeply held beliefs or motivations, most of us would be hard-pressed to clearly communicate how and why our behaviors are driven by them—we are ignorant of ourselves, goes the common adage. So what might account for this difference between our two dads in question if not age, income or generational location? Using a microcultures lens, we'd be able to see that the first dad is a progressive type who believes in sharing household duties with his wife. We also learn that he is scared of the long-term negative impact of the industrialized food production system. As a result, he chooses natural and organic products for his child. In terms of the second dad, we find that his entire beliefs framework is different, thereby accounting for his disregard of organic foods. This dad has a more traditional, conservative belief system, which impacts his household in that he leaves food purchasing (and all other domestic) decisions to his wife. She is the one who decides what their child eats, and he is mostly oblivious to her choices.

With a beliefs-driven model, we are able to get to the heart of these different dads' consumption behaviors by first making sense

---

[199] Scott Berinato, "The Demographics of Cool," *Harvard Business Review,* December 2011, https://hbr.org/2011/12/the-demographics-of-cool.

of their beliefs and then making sense of the symbolic capital that drives them. While this may seem like a lackluster example when we take just two dads into account, think of the explanatory, in-depth implications of an approach that could discern hundreds of thousands, if not millions of such nuanced differences. Once we are able to understand the symbolic capital that drives the behaviors of different consumers, we become armed with the information necessary to explain who is going to drive the mainstream in the future. The microcultures approach thus solves the inherent *reliability problem* of demographics and generational-based thinking by going deeper and making sense of consumers' beliefs and, in turn, their unconscious and unmet needs.

Let's consider an actual example from our own research that further explains this link between consumers' belief systems and their choices, this time in regard to probiotics. How might someone's belief system explain their propensity for buying and using probiotic supplements? First, we determined that probiotic supplements sit in a microculture of longevity. Said otherwise, the dominant meanings around probiotics consumption have to do with prioritizing a long life. Then, we were able to identify how different types of people made sense of longevity in their own lives based on what they believed. Let's spell this out: There are those people who feel that the locus of control over longevity ultimately lies in their hands. We might think of this group of people as "interventionists," because they typically believe that their actions, behavior and life practices play a crucial role in extending their longevity and their ongoing potency. As a result, this group is most likely to purchase probiotic supplements if they feel it can help improve their quality of life and health. Then we might think of another group of people with a different set of beliefs, such as those having a more "resigned" orientation to life, believing that control over longevity ultimately lies outside of them—either in the hands of God or in the set of genetic traits they were born with. For people who think this way, it is quite unlikely that they would choose to spend their money on health-related products or make other sacrifices, since they consider their longevity to be out of their control and thus futile. A more middle-range belief on longevity could be thought of in terms of people who are "symptom-driven," that is, people whose relationship to their longevity is determined by their life circumstances or by the specific health challenges they face in a particular moment in time. These people might tackle certain issues or symptoms if they have them, but if not, they would not go out of their way to tend to their longevity. Hence, this group would only circumstantially be prone to consume something like probiotics. This example on probiotics and the microculture of longevity shows us how people's propensity for a particular behavior—buying and using probiotic supplements or products—is shaped by the relationship they have to their longevity and how that squares with their belief system.

Microcultures also equip us with the data necessary for placing a specific *value* on the demographics surrounding a trend. But we do this *after* we come to understand the context, and *after* we identify the symbolic capital defining the various microcultures and determining which microcultures are bigger, which are growing and which are shrinking.

But it is not easy for our clients to abandon their longstanding belief in demographic or generational thinking—no matter how strong our evidence to the contrary may be. For example, in the weeks following the Fair Oaks Farm scandal, we were still struggling to convince one of our dairy clients that consumers were increasingly considering animal welfare in their dairy-purchasing decisions. In this particular incident, our client was adamant that the dominant trend in dairy was still connected to people's concerns with health and tolerability. They had conducted a survey soon after the Fair Oaks Farm video had gone viral and found that the segment they cared most about, millennials, didn't actually know of or care about the issue that much. In contrast, our big data ethnography revealed another story altogether: a story that was clearly being corroborated by a reduction in Fairlife milk's sales growth rates and increasing sales of plant-based dairy alternatives.

What people say in a survey or in a focus group is often quite far removed from what they really believe because, as mentioned, it is inherently difficult (or undesirable) to communicate why we are driven by the symbolic capital around an issue. Remember our friend from Chapter One who was on a cleanse and not a diet? Or, what about the Mercedes driver who extols the virtues of his high-performance German engine to his friends when in fact, it's the glimmering and unmistakable Mercedes ornament on the front of his car that really gets his heart thumping with excitement?

Let's consider another example from one of our clients that again highlights the gaps in traditional demographic or generational thinking. Two years ago, we worked with a major cereal company. Like the majority of organizations, they conducted surveys and found out that people were still buying cereal, although sales were clearly going down. Industry reports and mainstream media analysts claimed the same thing: the sales of hot and cold cereals combined had been on a steady decline since 2009, with a drop in revenue upward of $2 billion.[200] What our client was also able to gather from their survey was *a pronounced shift in attitudes that varied across generational categories*: While millennials were no longer buying cereal, parents of teenagers (typically Gen Xers) were still buying it, as were an older demographic of people whose children had moved out (typically baby boomers or "empty nesters"). So, while the attitudes of younger people regarding breakfast cereals had changed, the attitudes of older people had not. The company therefore decided to no longer target young mothers as they had done in the past but instead maintain the status quo in terms of their product, not changing anything in terms of ingredients or packaging but simply shifting its focus to a new target demographic: people aged 45 and up. This is what we would call the classic segmentation frame.

However, when we came on board to offer additional consultation to this major cereal manufacturer (who was not doing well after having decided to shift its marketing strategy to an older audience of cereal eaters), we were able to see things quite a bit more clearly (and expansively) through our microculture lens. We found that cereal was actually sitting in a few microcultures that told a more nuanced

---

[200] James F. Peltz, "Why Americans Are Eating Less Cold Cereal for Breakfast," *Los Angeles Times*, October 10, 2016, https://www.latimes.com/business/la-fi-agenda-breakfast-cereals-20161010-snap-story.html.

story than the segmented model that our client had landed on via survey data. The cereal industry was being driven by a microculture of convenience, and the microculture that had been driving convenience had itself changed!

How so? The microculture of convenience was now ridden with guilt. People were uncomfortable associating with a product like cereal that was itself associated with convenience, which had also come to mean "unhealthy" in the eyes of many consumers. Another way of saying this is that the symbolic capital within the convenience microculture had shifted from positive to negative (i.e., from convenience as an advantage to convenience as a source of guilt, since it had come to be associated with processed foods, lazy parenting, and so on). In response to this rejection of convenient breakfast cereals, an emerging "DIY" breakfast microculture was emerging. This included a growing interest in eating overnight oats, which, although requiring preparation ahead of time, didn't actually amount to much work at all. This indicated to us that there was an emerging microculture of ease (a trend that is markedly different from convenience in that it was not associated with guilt or unhealthy ingredients). We also identified a growing focus on whole grain ingredients in a microculture of health as well as another emergent microculture around dairy-free breakfast options, which has given rise to breakfast cereal bars that don't require milk and can be eaten on-the-go.

Let's take a moment to summarize what we discerned through our big data ethnography and when viewing the cereal consumption landscape through a microculture lens: Traditional cereal is under threat by several emerging microcultures: (1) a microculture of convenience (mostly because convenience has come to be associated with guilt and unhealthy ingredients); (2) a microculture around ease of breakfast preparation, that includes DIY options; (3) a dairy-free microculture (which is still small but growing).

Now that we understood the various microcultures driving the breakfast cereal industry, we were *then* able to reliably assess the demographics constituting those microcultures at play. We saw, for example, a skew of younger parents on the new narrative around health, as well as a skew of younger people on the anti-milk narrative.

Doing things in this order—microculture(s) first, demographics second—reveals the extent to which consumer trends or cultural phenomena do not occur in isolation. What we are thus arguing is *not* that we need to ditch the segmentation model altogether, but that we need to modify it substantially so as to make the process of evaluating opportunities more reliable and rigorous. We call this *microsegmentation*, because we do not want to capture every consumer in a particular predefined category but instead aim to home in on the leading microculture or two.

In essence, we use microcultures as the underlying framework with which to build market strategies, rather than relying on archaic and creativity-limiting segmentation models.

Instead of looking at consumers as a number, in the cereal example our client began to ask if they understood the dominant beliefs that transcended age and generation. They started to push beyond an industry perspective to see if they had uncovered the *real* demand spaces by looking through the consumer's lens. Doing so allowed them to realize that there was potential in bringing *healthfulness* and a solution that was *a little less convenient* together to create a revised offering. This product reduced the guilt of excess convenience and gave the consumer the ability to "add value" to their cereal through a simple DIY process that also opened the door to consumer-led creativity and recipe creation.

As a result of the microcultures approach, our client was able to push themselves to embrace new solutions and new ways of thinking to be better aware of what was actually happening, as opposed to what the industry and traditional research told them was happening. This propelled the organization to make its senior and middle management aware of the consumer-led lens in their industry so they could say:

"This is water. It's holding us back."

The cereal case is an important example of how the rate of change in cultural trends can often catch business leaders off guard. And as we have seen in previous chapters, leaders can no longer rely on convenient or easy solutions if the goal is to separate their businesses from the competition and solve the innovation failure problem. Otherwise, like a fish unaware of its surroundings, they will get swept away in the current of progress.

CHAPTER SEVEN

The Death of the Billion-Dollar Brand and How the "Consumer Perspective" Will Shape the Road Ahead

Malcolm Gladwell's 2013 book *David and Goliath: Underdogs, Misfits, and the Art of Battling Giants* delivers an important message. No matter how confident you may be about your business, the rules of the game can change. Why? Because what we generally perceive as an advantage today, like say, Goliath's prowess and strength, can actually turn out to be a disadvantage in the not-so-distant future.

And vice versa.

Someone's small size and sheer will can lead to amazing results when it forces them to compensate for a perceived weakness. Like David, many businesses and brands around the world are much smaller than their competition. They embrace their size and choose to be exceptionally nimble. And in order to prevail, they are not facing the Goliaths of the world head on. Instead, they are changing the rules of the game by becoming highly agile and prioritizing the process of building empathy for their consumers (an approach that traditional businesses have historically never taken).

In this final chapter, we explore how this phenomenon is forcing billion-dollar brands to reimagine their role in the lives of consumers as they are being usurped by unassuming smaller businesses and start-ups. We will focus on two key changes in the marketplace: first, the globalization of production, and second, the emergence of e-commerce and related Internet technologies that have fundamentally changed the process of understanding and reaching consumers. And of course, we will examine the role microcultures can play to help larger companies compete effectively with these new, nimble competitors. It will enable them to better understand the fragmented spaces that make up a marketplace and identify those growing demand spaces that will become the greatest opportunities and the biggest threats.

The Rebooting of Globalization

During the nineteenth century, the integration of separate, specialized world regions of agricultural and industrial production started to reconfigure the way we connected with people, products and cultures around the world. Industrial technologies made the operation of factories more commonplace. The railway, telegraph and steamship connected people who were previously cut off from each other. As a result, the organizational technologies of modernity like bureaucracy, landownership, census operations, government statistics, national legal systems and more emerged to accommodate this evolution in how humans conduct life and business. Hence, this period saw not only separate world regions with their own distinctive economic specializations emerge, but also a single world of rules and regulations for the operation of the system.

Moreover, not only did small, independent groups become more interconnected with the world around them, but corporate giants emerged as well. Businesses that were once focused on a single market expanded to new markets. As their reach grew, they gained access to more resources, increasing their bandwidth and profit as well. Like a snowball rolling down the side of a snowy mountain, globalization gave birth to giants.

But over the past decade, we have entered a new era of globalization—one that enables smaller, independent businesses to compete in markets and categories that only a decade ago were monopolized by corporate Goliaths. To understand this shift, we must look to the East.

There's a reason why we all know the "Made in China" cliché. For decades, it has represented labor-intensive manufactured goods created for corporate giants. This started to change when China opened itself up to foreign markets in the late 1970s. Technically, it wasn't until the 1990s that the private sector began to outsource to the East and gain momentum. But as confidence in globalization grew, massive amounts of Western capital and intellectual property began to flow into emerging markets throughout Asia. This integration was largely embraced as a feel-good story, and for good reason. The integration of China into global markets helped lift a billion people out of poverty.

But few understood at the time how this would reshape the way we do business around the world. Not only did this create a billion new shoppers hungry to mimic the consumerism generally associated with the West. It also started to eliminate the barriers that prevented small and medium-sized businesses from accessing the manufacturing that had given corporate Goliaths the ability to scale and profit from the products they sold. The process of market liberalization led to China's emergence as the world's most important global exporter. As more and more big businesses leveraged the East, more infrastructure and logistics were put in place. As China secured a stranglehold on large corporations' labor supply, they began to turn their attention to small and medium-sized businesses as a key area for revenue growth—doing for the Davids what they had successfully done for the Goliaths.

Why was this shift so critical?

Due to this type of globalization, the *cost* of market entry for companies in pretty much *any* industry has dropped dramatically. That is, the barrier for small and medium-sized businesses to access the same resources, materials and labor as the corporate giants has all but entirely disappeared. In fact, a product that used to cost millions of dollars to conceptualize, design, prototype, manufacture and ship can now be brought to market for less than $100,000 (dependent on the product, obviously). This is what we refer to as the democratization of mass manufacturing. To understand this phenomenon further, let's look a bit deeper into the impact of outsourcing on the world around us.

Spending on outsourced services in the global market represented a $45.6 billion marketplace in the year 2000. It was $85.6 billion in 2018, doubling in less than two decades (with approximately 84.2% of the total value of these outsourcing deals coming from the US).[201] But there's an interesting nuance to these statistics.

A substantial portion of this growth is increasingly being driven by new entrants into the market. Unlike twenty years ago, companies of all shapes and sizes are now leveraging a global network of employees, suppliers and resources in order to maintain a more agile and streamlined business model. And the more this model increased in popularity, the more barriers have come down that used to prevent access due to geography, logistics or even red tape. Outsourcing is increasingly being positioned as a common practice—and it is fueling a wide variety of start-ups to disrupt the industries they operate within.

Consider this example—if you are an entrepreneur wanting to start a new line of vegan accessories, you can easily reach the same types of manufacturing facilities in China, Bangladesh, Vietnam, India, Indonesia, the Philippines or, increasingly, Latin America (Mexico in particular), where manufacturing costs are much lower. You can also get immediate access to necessary infrastructure to get a product made and distributed at a lower cost than in the United States. Suppliers overseas, recognizing the potential for increased revenue,

---

[201] E. Mazareanu, "Global Outsourcing Market Size 2000–2018," *Statista*, July 22, 2019, https://www.statista.com/statistics/189788/global-outsourcing-market-size/; Kartik Ramakrishnan, "Global IT-BPO Outsourcing Deals Analysis," *KPMG*, May 2018, https://assets.kpmg/content/dam/kpmg/in/pdf/2018/05/KPMG-Deal-Tracker-2017.pdf.

have become increasingly open to working with smaller businesses. Many are creating specific partnership programs in order to help start-ups and small businesses compensate for their size and lack of organizational girth. Moreover, these manufacturers feel more valued when they work with smaller companies. By helping a small business manufacture items in smaller quantities, they can function without becoming an assembly line of cheap and unskilled labor (more on this below).[202] This globalized approach has changed what it means to start a business in the US. Outsourcing is not just profitable; it is increasingly becoming the norm. In fact, almost 30% of US start-ups moved at least some part of their operations offshore in 2018.[203]

The more this becomes the norm, the more this legitimizes the practice and the more opportunities open up for outsourcing innovation to occur. As a result, countries like China are aggressively trying to promote new capabilities—like "incredible engineering prowess" in hardware.

> By taking their prototypes directly to manufacturers and taking a small seed round from those companies [in China], start-ups are able to tear down many of the barriers that continually plague Silicon Valley hardware companies. When the supplier has skin in the game, several interests align, as the potential profit-sharing from a start-up's success can be far beyond a nominal manufacturing margin. The supplier now has an incentive to keep production costs low, a disincentive to work with any competitors or abuse the IP, a sense of responsibility to maintain the highest quality controls, and an urgency to bring the product to market as quickly as possible.[204]

---

[202] Eli Harris, "China's Manufacturers Are Enabling a New Model of Startup Incubation," *Venture Beat*, October 15, 2017, https://venturebeat.com/2017/10/15/chinas-manufacturers-are-enabling-a-new-model-of-startup-incubation/.
[203] Silicon Valley Bank, "US Startup Outlook 2018: Startup Outlook Survey," 2018, https://www.svb.com/globalassets/library/uploadedfiles/content/trends_and_insights/reports/startup_outlook_report/us/svb-suo-us-report.pdf.
[204] Harris, "China's Manufacturers Are Enabling."

China is changing the traditional path of development we have grown accustomed to seeing and reading about in Silicon Valley. The Chinese government is dismantling previous foreign trade barriers in order to increase innovative areas of development, most notably in the realm of high skilled tasks in AI and in the collection of big data:

Recent reforms [in China] will make it easier for international start-ups to gain access to lucrative industries, including grain export, wholesale medicine, gas and oil exploration, mining, transportation, and manufacturing ... The underlying message to foreign start-ups, then, is one of welcome, with a chief selling point being that China will eventually offer them the most propitious launch pad in the world for their businesses.[205]

China is no longer the sweatshops of yesteryear. It is now a critical partner. Writing about how he started his portable energy start-up, EcoFlow, cofounder and CEO Eli Harris explains why he sought out a Chinese company as one of his key players in their supply chain:

They have incubated and guided our supply chain every step of the way, working with us, not for us. In less than 11 months we designed, developed, produced, and shipped 5,000 units of our first product, a sophisticated energy storage system, to 21 countries. We have also shipped a full range of accessories and are in pre-production for a second product launch; and we have hired more than 10 full-time employees.[206]

These changes in manufacturing culture (and the politics that govern it) enable an increasing number of Western-based small companies and start-ups to bring new products to market faster and for less money. And as the world notices how this symbiotic relationship thrives, we increasingly see other Asian and Latin American countries following suit.

---

[205] Harris, "China's Manufacturers Are Enabling."
[206] Harris, "China's Manufacturers Are Enabling."

But this new flexibility in how we build things is only half the equation. As we are sure you have seen, selling online allows a small business or start-up to connect directly with consumers (B2C) and eliminate the need for intermediary retailers. In fact, if you want to take a new idea from the lab to market, you will likely follow a path that didn't exist a mere twenty years ago. There is no need to finance a brick-and-mortar location or fight to get your product on an existing retailer's store shelves.

Instead, you will likely go straight to the web and sell your product on Amazon or other popular online marketplaces like Etsy, eBay, Shopify or even Craigslist.[207]

E-commerce presents entrepreneurs with more than just the speed and agility that makes innovative concepts viable. It means that anyone can be a potential threat and eventual competitor to your business. Because anyone, and we mean almost anyone, can come up with a concept, craft a narrative and put something into the market that can stand out and defy convention. This "leveling of the playing field" hasn't just led to challenger brands that have disrupted their respective multi-billion-dollar-a-year industries.[208] It has given rise to online platforms and marketplaces that have created a more direct channel for start-ups to sell to consumers.

Consider the success of Liberty Jane Clothing, a popular fashion

---

[207] Emily Dayton, "Amazon Statistics You Should Know: Opportunities to Make the Most of America's Top Online Marketplace," *Big Commerce*, no date, https://www.bigcommerce.com/blog/amazon-statistics/#amazon-everything-to-everybody. These are the top online sites for e-commerce, with Amazon being the largest and top e-commerce platform in the US—more than 197 million people worldwide visit the site *each month*. And it's worth noting that more than 50% of all Amazon sales come from third-party sellers, a rate that has been increasing steadily since 2013. See also J. Clement, "Preferred Online Marketplaces of U.S. Sellers 2019," *Statista*, August 9, 2019, https://www.statista.com/statistics/448892/leading-online-marketplaces-sellers-usa/.

[208] Etsy, "Economic Impact of U.S. Etsy Sellers," *Etsy Dashboards*, last updated February 27, 2019, https://dashboards.mysidewalk.com/etsy-economic-impact-1532038450. See also J. Clement, "Etsy: Number of Active Sellers 2012–2018," *Statista*, August 9, 2019, https://www.statista.com/statistics/409374/etsy-active-sellers/.

brand... for dolls. To get this business off the ground, the company leveraged a variety of online marketplaces before ultimately creating its own platform. The business started from Cinnamon and Jason Miles's home, when they were inspired by their six-year-old daughter's obsession with dolls. As a trained seamstress and designer, Cinnamon began creating clothes for her daughter's tiny imaginary friends and crafted them on an old sewing machine. When she realized how much attention the doll's outfits were getting from kids around the neighborhood, Cinnamon took her idea online and immediately started selling digitally downloadable doll patterns on eBay. At first, the start-up was earning about $1000 a month. Soon, her husband started spreading the word via marketing on social media. Just over ten years later, Cinnamon and her husband are running Pixie Fair, their own online store. It was last valued at over $10 million and is now the web's largest doll clothes pattern marketplace.[209]

Pixie Fair is but one example. As of 2018, more than 2.1 million sellers sold goods through the Etsy platform. They generated $4.7 billion. Most impressive is that "79% of the sellers on the site are microbusinesses with a single person, with 97% of them running their shops from their home."[210] Anyone can be an entrepreneur, and—as we can see in the Liberty Jane Clothing/Pixie Fair example—if you tap into a niche microculture that has an unmet need, it can generate millions. Of course, if you tap into a microculture that solves a monumental mainstream problem, it can generate billions and crush a corporate giant.

Look at the evolution of the Dollar Shave Club (DSC). The DSC is a B2C razor business that is available exclusively online and works by giving its consumers the ability to buy monthly subscription packages of razors and blade cartridges at a fraction of the retail cost of the same product. Cofounder Michael Dubin (a struggling improv actor), got things going from his Santa Monica apartment in 2016. Using $4500 of his own money, he created a YouTube explainer video for

---

[209] Tucker Schreiber, "How One Couple Is Making $600,000 Per Year Selling Digital Products," *Shopify Blogs*, March 11, 2015, https://www.shopify.ca/blog/17587420-how-one-couple-is-making-600-000-per-year-selling-digital-products.

[210] Etsy, "Economic Impact of U.S. Etsy Sellers." Microbusinesses are defined as those which have a maximum of ten employees.

his razor membership service—the first of its kind. Helped by some clever writing and well-placed swear words, the video immediately went viral. In its first year, the company earned $4 million in revenue and had 600,000 members. By the end of its second year, it had earned $19 million.[211] In July 2018, four years after it first launched, DSC was bought by Unilever for almost $1 billion and today, the company has four million members who receive a monthly or bimonthly package of razor blades or other personal-care products at their homes.

Part of the DSC success can be attributed to social media marketing that helped it create "an army of brand ambassadors" who endorse the company for free. With the money DSC saves in marketing costs, they are able to keep their prices low and extremely competitive, while big brands like Gillette are typically spending "billions for TV spot, brand ambassadors, and front-shelf placements in multiple stores."[212] DSC also saves overhead costs by purchasing its razors cheaply from suppliers in China and South Korea and then manages its inventory from a single distribution center.[213] Its biggest achievement, however? That it managed to go head-to-head with shaving giant Gillette, which had been *the* dominant contender in the razor blade market for *more than a century.*[214] While the Gillette brand still holds about 54% of the global market share for razors, that number is a significant drop from its 70% share in 2010.[215] The DSC newbie and the numerous other start-up shave clubs

[211] Breadnbeyond, "The $4,500 Investment that Turns Dollar Shave Club into a $1 Billion Company," *Medium*, March 20, 2017, https://medium.com/@breadnbeyond/the-4-500-investment-that-turns-dollar-shave-club-into-a-1-billion-company-b7f2b3b648a1.

[212] Breadnbeyond, "The $4,500 Investment."

[213] TradeGecko, "How Dollar Shave Club Dominates the Cutthroat World of eCommerce," *TradeGecko*, May 22, 2018, https://www.tradegecko.com/blog/small-business-growth/how-dollar-shave-club-dominates-ecommerce.

[214] Ciara Linnane, "Proctor & Gamble's Gillette Razor Business Dinged by Online Shave Clubs," *MarketWatch*, April 27, 2017, https://www.marketwatch.com/story/procter-gambles-gillette-razor-business-dinged-by-online-shave-clubs-2017-04-26.

[215] Kaitlin Tiffany, "The Absurd Quest to Make the 'Best' Razor," *Vox*, December 11, 2018, https://www.vox.com/the-goods/2018/12/11/18134456/

it has inspired (e.g., Harry's) has largely been responsible for this disruption. Reflecting on the "creative destruction" embodied by the DSC business model, an article in the *New York Times* concludes that "the very nature of a company is fundamentally changing, becoming smaller and leaner with far fewer employees."[216]

This would not have been possible twenty years ago:

> In the past ... [i]t would have required billions of dollars to invest in a distribution network and advertising to get the product on store shelves. No more. Now you can get free advertising through YouTube, easy distribution through the mail system and low-cost sales through the Internet. Factories and distribution can be bolted on throughout the globe.[217]

Globalization and e-commerce have flooded the market with more products and solutions than ever before, and this has created an unprecedented level of choice for the everyday consumer. More options mean more fragmentation. As we will see next, this shift has ushered in the age of belief-based consumption.

How E-commerce Is Driving Us to Buy Based on Beliefs and Values

We are not the first to compare the Internet to Gutenberg's printing press. Nor will we likely be the last. But in the context of making information flow more easily and taking the power from the few and putting it in the hands of the masses, the metaphor seems apt. Like the printing press that democratized reading and the ability to access information, the Internet has democratized knowledge gathering and given more people access to information, culture and products from

---

best-razor-gillette-harrys-dollar-shave-club.

[216] Steven Davidoff Solomon, "$1 Billion for Dollar Shave Club: Why Every Company Should Worry," *New York Times*, July 26, 2016, https://www.nytimes.com/2016/07/27/business/dealbook/1-billion-for-dollar-shave-club-why-every-company-should-worry.html.

[217] Solomon, "$1 Billion for Dollar Shave Club."

around the globe. This is especially true when you consider the impact of e-commerce. In a matter of minutes, you can learn that a product exists, "Google" how it is made and what it stands for, find an online portal where it is sold and have it express-shipped to your doorstep in less than twenty-four hours.

This fundamental shift in how we choose "what to buy" is critical to understanding the importance of microcultures. More choice has made us pickier. It has transformed how we make decisions and how we choose to legitimize or justify them (see Chapter Two). Our everyday choices are shaped by our beliefs more than ever before, and this has led to the birth of numerous microcultures and numerous forms of symbolic capital that compete for power and prestige. Decisions like what type of razor you buy, how you buy it, how you use it and even how you choose to dispose of it all generate varying forms of symbolic capital and create multiple microcultures within which numerous businesses, both big and small, already operate. Increased choices and smaller barriers to launch have led to increased fragmentation of markets, with the smaller players really focused on targeting, often unknowingly, a specific microculture.

All this has of course fundamentally changed our expectations as consumers. We want to feel like our consumerism is tailored to our very specific needs. We want our shopping carts to tell the story of us. We want to vote with our wallets and create meaning with our purchases. What we buy says something about who we are. Therefore, we grow increasingly strategic about what we buy. The pickier we become as consumers, the more choice and variation we demand. We can see this in the grocery aisle. According to economist James Besser, the average grocery store now carries about fifty times more products than it did eighty years ago. And market research firm Mintel says that the number of new packaged goods introduced to the market every year has increased thirtyfold since the 1970s.[218]

But this doesn't mean that consumers just want "new" slapped on the front of the product they are buying. As you can imagine, it is more

---

[218] Christoper Mims, "Why There Are More Consumer Goods Than Ever," *Wall Street Journal*, April 25, 2016, https://www.wsj.com/articles/why-there-are-more-consumer-goods-than-ever-1461556860.

complicated than this. Consumers want to feel like they are doing something meaningful, even when it comes to quenching their thirst.

In the early 1980s, if you asked someone who Coca-Cola was competing with, the answer was clear: Pepsi. Today, Coca-Cola has to compete with an ever-growing landscape of nonalcoholic beverage companies and brands, including everything from organic colas to bottled water to flavored waters, coconut water, sports and energy drinks and more. Don't take our word for it:

> Twenty years ago, competition in the consumer products industry looked like professional tennis. You faced opponents with business models that were similar to yours. You had been playing against them for years. It was tough but predictable and manageable. Now, the competition resembles mixed martial arts. Players come from every sport. Products and brands expand into adjacent territories in an effort to cater to *more consumer needs.* Retailers have essentially become competitors through their expanded private label offerings. And small insurgent companies out-innovate and out-hustle large established firms, eroding their share in most premium segments.[219]

Consumers today prefer brands that are new, innovative and small[220] because new, innovative and small brands often provide the consumer with more than the product itself. They tap into a microculture that shares values with the brand, so you don't feel like you are buying a product. You are buying what the product represents. We can see this clearly happening in the shoe industry, for example.

When Allbirds—the San Francisco–based sneakers start-up—entered the market, they made it very clear that their shoes were unbelievably comfortable. But they challenged the norms in footwear

---

[219] Matthew Meacham et al., "Overcoming the Existential Crisis in Consumer Goods," *Bain & Company*, March 7, 2018, https://www.bain.com/insights/overcoming-the-existential-crisis-in-consumer-goods/ (emphasis added).

[220] Solomon, "$1 Billion for Dollar Shave Club."

by creating a relatively limited number of minimalistic designs to live up to a promise: that every shoe would be constructed with natural, environmentally friendly materials like merino wool and eucalyptus tree fiber. And in a category where volume is often driven by discounting, Allbirds stands for something more. At the time of writing this book, if you Googled "Allbirds" and "Discount Code," you were directed to this:

> At Allbirds, we don't believe in discounts. Why, you ask? Because we work hard everyday to make premium-quality shoes that look great and feel amazing (think cashmere sweater, but for your feet!)—all while minimizing our impact on the planet and cost to you. That's the beauty of selling directly to our fans![221]

Take that Nike. Take that Adidas. Take that Walmart, or Foot Locker. You are not making the rules anymore. Allbirds sells directly to consumers and is now valued at $1.4 billion.[222]

From clothes for dolls and a subscription to a razor service to a more sustainable shoe, the game has changed. So if your company is a Goliath and you want to survive, you don't just need to embrace the fragmentation. You need to embrace microcultures to anticipate where and when your company might be exposed to threats and opportunities and transform your organization's thinking from an industry-led mindset to one that is consumer-led.

The Danger of Building Billion-Dollar Brands

The Fortune 1000 needs to reimagine what is worth bringing to market and what they define as "too small" an opportunity. Until recently, top companies like Procter & Gamble (P&G) and Unilever used to make a

---

[221] Allbirds, "What's Our Deal?" *Allbirds*, 2019, https://www.allbirds.ca/pages/truth-about-allbirds-coupons.

[222] Tom Huddleston Jr., "How Allbirds Went from Silicon Valley Fashion Staple to a $1.4 Billion Sneaker Start-Up," *CNBC*, December 18, 2018, https://www.cnbc.com/2018/12/14/allbirds-went-from-silicon-valley-staple-to-billion-sneaker-startup.html.

large portion of their overall revenue from a handful of major brands. But in the age of microcultures, these companies will have to host a *multitude* of brands to satisfy the varied tastes of the consumer and sustain their size and competitiveness. P&G, for example, carries well over twenty popular name brands and a number of less popular ones.[223]

As markets become more fragmented and as more and more microcultures proliferate, big companies have no choice but to play the game of diversification. They can either innovate and introduce their own new brands or increase their brand acquisitions. But most importantly, they need to stop following industry trends and making assumptions based on an industry perspective. Instead, they need to embrace the beliefs and values of the consumer (even if it defies rational reasoning) and ask themselves, "Are we approaching this from the consumer's perspective?" This is why the concept of microcultures is so important.

Consumers no longer want "something for everyone." Building for the mainstream is a recipe for banality and ubiquity. The brands that will thrive begin by aligning themselves to the beliefs and values of a microculture. This microculture will, in time, change how macrocultures think about the category itself. This is why it is imperative that senior leadership not only study and understand microcultures but also feed them with their innovations, so they can ride the tide of change instead of swimming against it.

Why "buy" the competition when you can beat them?

In 2018, for example, Coca-Cola purchased a small Australian kombucha label, Organic & Raw Trading Co., which makes the MOJO brand of naturally fermented kombucha drinks.[224] The company has also invested in or acquired other "natural" labels, such as Honest Tea, Suja Juice (organic and non-GMO) and ZICO Coconut Water—mostly because it, along with the rest of the carbonated soft drink industry, was being criticized for the negative health consequences of high sugar content. Rather than coming up with its own version of

---

[223] Investopedia, "Who Are Procter & Gamble's Main Competitors?" *Investopedia*, May 7, 2019, https://www.investopedia.com/ask/answers/120114/who-are-proctor-gambles-pg-main-competitors.asp.

[224] Coca-Cola Company, "Coca-Cola Adds First Line of Kombucha."

a low-sugar or healthy beverage, Coca-Cola bought already existing ones.[225]

In 2014, General Mills acquired the natural and organic food brand Annie's. The merger of these two companies means that the smaller one, Annie's, has been able to leverage General Mills's significant manufacturing and technical resources, the company's knowledge and business experience and its category management and robust sales capabilities.[226] And for General Mills, the acquisition of Annie's along with a number of other natural and organic brands (e.g., EPIC, Lärabar, Food Should Taste Good and Cascadian Farms) has also meant a number of advantages that go beyond profit alone.

As explained by Steve Young, a vice president at General Mills:
> What we've really learned is the speed-to-market; when you are truly mission- and purpose-driven, it gives you a lens for every decision you make, and you can make them fast when that's the case ... We move faster. In the past, we may have said, "Well, we'd better research this; we'd better test this." What we're doing now is saying, "We know this is right. We're going to go."[227]

The list of big-name companies that have adapted to the burgeoning of natural, organic and ethical microcultures in this way—from food and beverages to personal-care and beauty products—is a long one.

In addition to Coca-Cola and General Mills, a slew of other major companies have acquired smaller, more natural or ethical ones: Burt's Bees was bought by Clorox for almost $1 billion in 2011; Ben & Jerry's ice cream was bought for $326 million by Unilever in 2000; the natural personal-care product label Tom's of Maine was bought by

---

[225] Monika Watrous, "Coke Learns Big Lessons from Small Startups," *Food Business News*, March 18, 2016, https://www.foodbusinessnews.net/articles/7577-coke-learns-big-lessons-from-small-startups.

[226] Monika Watrous, "When Big Companies Buy Small Brands," *Food Business News*, March 14, 2016, https://www.foodbusinessnews.net/articles/7712-when-big-companies-buy-small-brands.

[227] Watrous, "When Big Companies Buy Small Brands."

Colgate-Palmolive for $100 million in 2006; L'Oréal bought The Body Shop for $1.1 billion in 2006; and PepsiCo bought Naked Juice for $540 million, also in 2006.

All these acquisitions represent brands that appealed to a microculture and, in time, started to impact and reshape the expectations of the mainstream or macroculture. They were not just bought because of the revenue they could generate for the buyer. They represent something that the buyer was failing to deliver to their consumers. The buyer missed the boat. And it cost them.

Why do companies miss the boat? In Chapter Six, we went to great lengths explaining the problem with traditional research methods, particularly those that rely heavily on generational frameworks and demographic characteristics. We also explained that such frameworks exist because they are easy to use for middle management—they fit into the industry-led mind-set that senior leadership leverages in order to drive business targets and measure results. This means that, despite knowing how toxic such frameworks can be to the success of innovation projects, middle management constantly falls back on such traditional frameworks so as to minimize the hassle of "managing up." This is the prime reason why larger companies struggle so much with innovation and why they're always late to the game. As a result, instead of building "the next big thing," they resort to making bloated acquisition and investment decisions in order to save their stock from tumbling.

It's not that smaller companies are better at leveraging social-sciences-based frameworks that makes them more innovative. Not at all. We certainly don't see any difference between smaller and larger companies in the adoption rate of the microcultures framework. The difference simply lies in the fact that in highly innovative, smaller companies—like DSC and Pixie Fair—the leader is innately (just through gut feeling) building products and solutions to cater to a specific microculture. Because these companies are small and often privately owned, with a small group of key stakeholders, such decisions can be made quickly and mistakes can be rectified just as easily. Companies don't enjoy this luxury when they start to grow and add on investors, shareholders, senior leaders, hundreds of employees, etc.

Here's an interesting observation we've made after working closely with senior leadership across companies big and small. The moment revenue surpasses about $100 million, the innate "gut feeling" that led to the first $100 million begins to dissolve from the fabric of the organization. It is taken over by the same kind of industry-led frameworks and mind-sets that large corporations suffer from.

Of course, there are exceptions to this rule, but having now worked with hundreds of different companies over the last decade, we can say with confidence that such exceptions are few and far between.

In the process of writing this book, we spoke to hundreds of executives across more than two hundred Fortune 1000 companies. Our goal was to try and understand *why* the allure of industry-led frameworks was so strong among senior management. After many hours of conversation, some casual and some more formal, we noticed a pattern that led us back to the first time we thought about our mission as a company. Let us elaborate.

Corporations Bet on Cultural Homogenization

Most executives misunderstand the impact of globalization on culture, and there is historical precedence and significance to why they think this way. But more on that later. Most believe that because of the hyperconnected nature of our world today, human beings are becoming more alike. That is, they believe that our cultures are converging or gradually becoming more and more homogenized. It is for this reason that they feel more than comfortable assuming that a generation feels and acts a certain way. It is for the same reason that they feel very comfortable assuming that a family in a life stage (e.g., with children under the age of five) will think, act and feel the same way. And it is for the same reason that they feel even more comfortable believing that the future of any product or industry or trend is being shaped by younger people, especially those under the age of 30.

All these assumptions, as discussed in detail in Chapter Six, exist because—whether knowingly or unknowingly—these leaders have been trained to believe that our culture is becoming gradually homogenized, not diversified.

However, if there's one thing that the microcultures framework and research methodology has taught us, it's that the truth is far from this presumed reality. If our culture was in fact getting homogenized, that is, if we were all starting to make similar choices, then we wouldn't be seeing an unprecedented rise in start-ups that have carved out niche markets for themselves. We also wouldn't be seeing the decline of Goliath brands, and we certainly would not be experiencing the desire, as people and as consumers, to acquire the myriad forms of symbolic capital that could give us the power and prestige over our peers, be it in our personal or professional lives. The truth is, our culture has never been more diverse. More importantly, it has to be said that for as long as the field of cultural anthropology has existed, culture has always been observed as something that is diversifying, not homogenizing.

In the early twentieth century, while Margaret Mead and Franz Boas were defining the parameters of cultural anthropology as a whole new field of study, the prevailing assumption of the time was that different cultural groups should be viewed hierarchically, in that some groups were lagging behind—so-called primitives—while others, generally those in the Western world, had "succeeded" at becoming "civilized." French anthropologist Claude Lévi-Strauss was one of the major proponents of this worldview. He argued that it was only a matter of time before the more "civilized" groups would influence the rest and, as a result, a homogeneous world culture would eventually prevail. Lévi-Strauss even went as far as to suggest that, "the word 'anthropology' should be changed to 'entropology'—the study of the homogenization of human life across the planet."[228]

"Cultural anthropology was the West's way of memorializing its victims" (where the victims, according to Lévi-Strauss, were the

---

[228] Louis Menand, "How Cultural Anthropologists Redefined Humanity," *New Yorker*, August 19, 2019, https://www.newyorker.com/magazine/2019/08/26/how-cultural-anthropologists-redefined-humanity.

"barbaric" and "primitive" cultures of the Global South who would eventually be absorbed into the more "civilized" cultures of the Western world).[229]

By contrast, Mead, Boas and the other anthropologists in their entourage emphasized that we live in a world composed of a multitude of cultural groups, all with their own practices, perspectives, insights and deficiencies—and each worthwhile in its own right. They did not view the world as a battleground between "barbarian" and "civilized" cultures, as Lévi-Strauss did, but rather studied foreign cultures as a "looking glass" of sorts: as a way of learning about how other groups lead their lives in order to better understand (and perhaps modify) their own Western practices and beliefs. The underlying point of this school of thought was to challenge the notion that the world was moving toward homogenization (as per Lévi-Strauss) and instead was a veritable cornucopia of human cultures living alongside one another—a fact that would only escalate as time moved forward.

For almost a century now, we've been drawing on the tenets of cultural anthropology to recognize and interpret the extent to which the world we live in is in a constant state of diversification, especially as evermore cultural groups become mobile (more often than not out of necessity) and hit up against one another in the process. To put it simply— we live in a time of extreme diversity, where multitudes of different cultural groups interact with and inevitably influence each other.

While cultural anthropology has been talking about this for the last one hundred years, it is primarily in the last ten to twenty years— with the advent of the Internet and social media—that we have seen such cultural diversification explode. This, in turn, has led to the ever-increasing fragmentation of markets as we become exposed to more ideas, products and brands that can more easily access geographically dispersed consumers.

This brings us back full circle.

If consumer culture becomes increasingly diverse and markets fragment while companies and their leaders continue to use practices

---

[229] Menand, "How Cultural Anthropologists Redefined Humanity."

that assume the opposite, this creates a fundamental disconnect between why a company does what it does and why people buy that company's products and solutions. This inevitably increases competition and disperses consumer loyalty.

All the design thinking and empathy-building projects in the world can't save a company in this position from being constantly left behind. This is the challenge that microcultures help solve, and it's not just relevant to the Fortune 1000. It's also pertinent to all those companies that are in "growth mode" and under threat of losing their "gut feeling" along the way.

If senior leadership (especially c-suite) takes the industry-led lens, it inadvertently signals to everyone who works there that "we see the world through a less diverse lens." It prevents the embrace of cultural fragmentation, which also means it prevents the embrace of the diverse range of mind-sets and opportunities that emerge in culture every single day. The industry-led lens doesn't just restrict an organization's ability to innovate from a process and operational standpoint; it also restricts its intellectual capacity to innovate. It makes the company close-minded and disconnects it from the reality of the marketplace.

This is why we believe this book couldn't have come at a better time. We now live in a world where dealing with complexity is a huge challenge for organizations big and small. Just think back to the Fair Oaks Farm example we started the book with.

The value of the microcultures framework is that it provides a learnable, teachable, repeatable and, most importantly, scalable solution for organizations to get past the industry-led lens and enter the world of consumer centricity. It teaches organizations to truly embrace the diversity of the marketplace and dispel age-old assumptions about certain "types" of consumers who are "too niche" or "too out there." It also enables organizations to act with the agility needed to think like the "Davids" in their industry and create solutions for influential microcultures (shaping the future of the macroculture) that would otherwise not have been discovered or would have been considered too "niche" for the business.

Last, and perhaps most importantly, using the microcultures

framework across the organization will make you feel good about the decisions you make as a leader.

Why?

Because it creates natural empathy for the diverse mind-sets, beliefs and forms of symbolic capital that make people who and what they are. It opens the door for leaders and teams to begin to think in a manner that is much more nuanced and, most importantly, aligned with the consumer. Recently, one of our newer clients—who has been working with us for just over nine months—told us that they finally put an end to their organization-wide "Hispanic strategy." Instead, they now embrace the reality of microcultures. They understand and see the world through that lens—one that looks at culture as being made up of a mix of people from different backgrounds, who come together because of the shared forms of capital they create and leverage in society. The result? Sales growth of over 450% in the last quarter and a 100% increase in their innovation success rate.

That's the power of microcultures.

Special thanks to Dr. Nadine Blumer for all her research
and input, throughout the process of writing this book.

Cover art by: Joe Borges R.G.D. Pomegranate Letterpress + Design

BIBLIOGRAPHY

Abercombie, Nicholas, Stephen Hill, and Bryan S. Turner. *The Penguin Dictionary of Sociology*, 4th ed. London, UK: Penguin, 1984.

Allbirds. "What's Our Deal?" *Allbirds*, 2019. https://www.allbirds.ca/pages/truth-about-allbirds-coupons.

Alony, Eyal. 2019. "The Adventure Series Makes an MRI Fun for Kids." *Parentology*, May 20, 2019. https://parentology.com/the-adventure-series-makes-mri-fun-for-kids/.

American Psychological Association. "Work Stress." *American Psychological Association*, no date. http://www.apaexcellence.org/resources/special-topics/work-stress.

Association of MBAs. "The March of the Sharing Economy." *Association of MBAs*, February 15, 2019. https://www.mbaworld.com/blogs-and-articles/the-march-of-the-sharing-economy.

Bacevice, Peter, Gretchen Spreitzer, Hilary Hendricks, and Daniel Davis. "How Coworking Spaces Affect Employees' Professional Identities." *Harvard Business Review*, April 17, 2019. https://hbr.org/2019/04/how-coworking-spaces-affect-employees-professional-identities.

Baumann, Shyon, and Josee Johnston. *Foodies: Democracy and Distinction in the Gourmet Foodscape*. New York: Routledge, 2009.

Beaton, Caroline. "6 Millennial Myths That Need to Finally Die." *Forbes*, September 6, 2016. https://www.forbes.com/sites/carolinebeaton/2016/09/06/6-millennial-myths-that-need-to-finally-die/#2c1453684fa0.

Bellon, Tina. "California Jury Hits Bayer with $2 Billion Award in Roundup Cancer Trial." *Reuters*, May 13, 2019. https://www.reuters.com/article/us-bayer-glyphosate-lawsuit/california-jury-hits-bayer-with-2-billion-award-in-roundup-cancer-trial-idUSKCN1SJ29F.

Belyh, Anastasia. "An Introduction to Sharing Economy." *Cleverism*, March 5, 2015. https://www.cleverism.com/introduction-to-sharing-economy/.

Benjamin, Jennifer. "Foodie Culture and Its Impact on the Culinary Landscape," *Lightspeed HQ*, last modified June 23, 2016. https://www.lightspeedhq.com/blog/foodie-culture-impact/.

Berger, Peter L. *Invitation to Sociology: A Humanistic Perspective*. New York: Doubleday, 1963.

Berger, Peter L., and Thomas Luckmann. *The Social Construction of Reality: A Treatise in the Sociology of Knowledge*. New York: Doubleday, 1966.

Berinato, Scott. "The Demographics of Cool." *Harvard Business Review*, December 2011. https://hbr.org/2011/12/the-demographics-of-cool.

Bialik, Kristen. "Key Facts about Race and Marriage, 50 Years after Loving v. Virginia." *Pew Research Center*, June 12, 2017. https://www.pewresearch.org/fact-tank/2017/06/12/key-facts-about-race-and-marriage-50-years-after-loving-v-virginia/.

Bialik, Kristen, and Richard Fry. "Millennial Life: How Young Adulthood Today Compares with Prior Generations." *Pew Research Center*, February 14, 2019. https://www.pewsocialtrends.org/essay/

millennial-life-how-young-adulthood-today-compares-with-pr
ior-generations/.

Blackburn, Inez. "Speed to Market—Capitalizing on Demand."
PowerPoint presentation, U Connect 08 conference, Gaylord Texan
Resort, Dallas, June 9–12, 2008. http://www.markettechniques.
com/assets/pdf/Speed2Market.pdf.

Blumer, Herbert. *Symbolic Interactionism: Perspective and Method.*
Englewood Cliffs, NJ: Prentice-Hall, 1969.

Bourdieu, Pierre. "The Forms of Capital." In *Handbook of Theory and
Research for the Sociology of Education*, edited by J.G. Richarson, 241–
58. New York: Greenwood Press, 1986.

Breadnbeyond. "The $4,500 Investment that Turns Dollar Shave
Club into a $1 Billion Company." *Medium*, March 20, 2017. https://
medium.com/@breadnbeyond/the-4-500-investment-that-turns-
dollar-shave-club-into-a-1-billion-company-b7f2b3b648a1.

Broadbent, Andrew. "Why Big Corporations Are Moving into
Coworking Spaces." *Entrepreneur*, January 22, 2018. https://web.
archive.org/web/20180613161436/https://www.entrepreneur.
com/article/307085.

Brown, Tim. "Design Thinking." *Harvard Business Review*, June 2008.
https://hbr.org/2008/06/design-thinking.

Bump, Philip. "Your Generational Identity Is a Lie." *Washington Post*,
April 1, 2015. https://www.washingtonpost.com/news/the-fix/
wp/2015/04/01/your-generational-identity-is-a-lie/.

BusinessWire. "Global Household Cleaning Products Market 2018–
2022." *BusinessWire*, September 7, 2018. https://www.businesswire.
com/news/home/20180907005520/en/Global-Household-Cleanin
g-Products-Market-2018-2022-Surface.

BusinessWire. "Global Male Grooming Products Market 2018–2023." *BusinessWire*, September 10, 2018. https://www.businesswire.com/news/home/20180910005394/en/Global-Male-Grooming-Products-Market-2018-2023—.

Camilli, Sascha. "H&M Launches Collection Made with Vegan Pineapple Leather and Orange Silk." *Plant Based News (PBN)*, April 1, 2019. https://www.plantbasednews.org/lifestyle/h-m-collection-vegan-pineappple-leather-orange-silk.

Captain, Sean. "The Demographics of Occupy Wall Street." *Fast Company*, October 19, 2011. https://www.fastcompany.com/1789018/demographics-occupy-wall-street.

Cardellino, Carly. "CoverGirl Announces Its First Male CoverGirl Spokesmodel." *Marie Claire*, October 11, 2016. https://www.marieclaire.com/beauty/a23038/male-covergirl-james-charles/.

Chai, Carmen. "Kraft Dinner to Remove Synthetic Colours by 2016, Company Says," *Global News*, April 20, 2015. https://globalnews.ca/news/1949205/kraft-dinner-to-remove-synthetic-colours-by-2016-company-says/.

Chanda, Nayan, and Susan Froetschel. *A World Connected: Globalization in the 21ˢᵗ Century.* New Haven, CT: Yale University Press, 2012.

Chang, YoungJoong, Jaibeom Kim, and Jaewoo Joo. "An Exploratory Study on the Evolution of Design Thinking: Comparison of Apple and Samsung." *Design Management Journal* 8, no. 1 (2013): 22–34.

Chappell, Bill. "Occupy Wall Street: From a Blog Post to a Movement." *National Public Radio (NPR)*, October 20, 2011. https://www.npr.org/2011/10/20/141530025/occupy-wall-street-from-a-blog-post-to-a-movement.

Charles, Vincent, and Tatiana Gherman. "Big Data Analytics and Ethnography: Together for the Greater Good." In *Big Data for the*

Greater Good: Studies in Big Data vol. 42, edited by Ali Emrouznejad and Charles Vincent, 19–33. Cham, Switzerland: Springer, 2018.

Cherry, Kendra. "How Confirmation Bias Works." *VeryWell Mind*, last modified September 8, 2019. https://www.verywellmind.com/what-is-a-confirmation-bias-2795024.

Chin, Nathan. "CoWorking with Wisdom Opens in Downtown Berkeley." *Daily Californian*, July 19, 2018. https://www.dailycal.org/2018/07/19/coworking-wisdom-opens-downtown-berkeley-providing-space-work-life-balance/.

Cills, Hazel. "A Short History of Manly Beauty Products for Masculine Men." *Jezebel*, June 19, 2019. https://jezebel.com/a-short-history-of-manly-beauty-products-for-masculine-1834956610.

Cilluffo, Anthony, and Richard Fry. "Gen Z, Millennials and Gen X Outvoted Older Generations in 2018 Midterms." *Pew Research Center*, May 29, 2019. https://www.pewresearch.org/fact-tank/2019/05/29/gen-z-millennials-and-gen-x-outvoted-older-generations-in-2018-midterms/.

Clement, J. "Etsy: Number of Active Sellers 2012–2018." *Statista*, August 9, 2019. https://www.statista.com/statistics/409374/etsy-active-sellers/.

Clement, J. "Number of Internet Users Worldwide 2005–2018." *Statista*, January 9, 2019. https://www.statista.com/statistics/273018/number-of-internet-users-worldwide/.

Clement, J. "Number of Global Social Network Users 2010–2021." *Statista*, August 14, 2019. https://www.statista.com/statistics/278414/number-of-worldwide-social-network-users/.

Clement, J. "Preferred Online Marketplaces of U.S. Sellers 2019." *Statista*, August 9, 2019. https://www.statista.com/statistics/448892/leading-online-marketplaces-sellers-usa/.

Clement, J. "Share of U.S. Population with a Social Media Profile 2008-2019." *Statista*, August 9, 2019. https://www.statista.com/statistics/273476/percentage-of-us-population-with-a-social-network-profile/.

Clement, J. "Social Media, Global Penetration Rate 2019, by Region." *Statista*, February 5, 2019. https://www.statista.com/statistics/269615/social-network-penetration-by-region/.

Coca-Cola Company. "Coca-Cola Adds First Line of Kombucha through Acquisition of Australian-based Organic & Raw Trading Co." *Coca-Cola Company*, September 19, 2018. https://www.coca-colacompany.com/stories/the-coca-cola-company-adds-its-first-line-of-kombucha-through-ac.

Conway, Jan. "Consumers Who Are Vegan or Vegetarian in the U.S. 2018, by Age Group." *Statista*, August 9, 2019. https://www.statista.com/statistics/738851/vegan-vegetarian-consumers-us/.

Cosmetics Business. "Cosmetics Business Reveals the Top 5 Trends Disrupting Men's Care in New Report." *Cosmetics Business*, April 10, 2019. https://www.cosmeticsbusiness.com/news/article_page/Cosmetics_Business_reveals_the_top_5_trends_disrupting_mens_care_in_new_report/153663.

Costanza, David P., Jessica M. Badger, Rebecca L. Fraser, Jamie B. Severt, and Paul A. Gade. "Generational Differences in Work-Related Attitudes: A Meta-analysis." *Journal of Business Psychology* 27, no. 4 (December 2012): 375–94.

Cowan, Robin, Bulat Sanditov, and Rifka Weehuizen. "Productivity Effects of Innovation, Stress and Social Relations." *Journal of Economic Behavior & Organization* 79 (2011): 165–182.

"Coworking." *Wikipedia*. Accessed July 19, 2019. https://en.m.wikipedia.org/wiki/Coworking.

Crockett, Zachary. "The Man Who Invented Scotch Tape." *Priceonomics*, December 30, 2014. https://priceonomics.com/the-man-who-invented-scotch-tape/.

Cusumano, Michael A. "The Sharing Economy Meets Reality." *Communications of the ACM* 61, no. 1 (2018): 26–28. https://cacm.acm.org/magazines/2018/1/223874-the-sharing-economy-meets-reality/abstract.

Dam, Rikke, and Teo Siang. "What Is Design Thinking and Why Is it So Popular?" *Interaction Design Foundation*, September 2019. https://www.interaction-design.org/literature/article/what-is-design-thinking-and-why-is-it-so-popular.

Day, Jessica. "The Impact of Stress on Innovation." *Ideascale*, July 10, 2018. https://ideascale.com/impact-of-stress-on-innovation/.

Dayton, Emily. "Amazon Statistics You Should Know: Opportunities to Make the Most of America's Top Online Marketplace." *Big Commerce*, no date. https://www.bigcommerce.com/blog/amazon-statistics/#amazon-everything-to-everybody.

DeBare, Ilana. "Shared Work Spaces a Wave of the Future." *SFGate*, February 19, 2008. https://www.sfgate.com/bayarea/article/Shared-work-spaces-a-wave-of-the-future-3294193.php#item-85307-tbla-3.

Devaney, Susan. "Lady Gaga's Latest All-Black Ensemble Is Vegan Leather." *Vogue*, July 19, 2019. https://www.vogue.co.uk/article/lady-gaga-leather-dress-boots.

Diamant, Jeff, and Besheer Mohamed. "Black Millennials Are More Religious Than Other Millennials." *Pew Research Center*, July 20, 2018. https://www.pewresearch.org/fact-tank/2018/07/20/black-millennials-are-more-religious-than-other-millennials/.

Dillon, Karen. "I Think of My Failures as a Gift." *Harvard Business Review,* April 2011. https://hbr.org/2011/04/i-think-of-my-failures-as-a-gift.

Dorst, Kees. *Frame Innovation: Create New Thinking by Design.* Cambridge, MA: MIT Press, 2012.

Douglas, Jack D. *Investigative Social Research: Individual and Team Field Research.* Beverly Hills, CA.: Sage Publications, 1976.

Drakopoulou Dodd, Sarah, Juliette Wilson, Ciáran Mac an Bhaird, and Angelo P. Bisignano. "Habitus Emerging: The Development of Hybrid Logics and Collaborative Business Models in the Irish Craft Beer Sector." *International Small Business Journal: Researching Entrepreneurship* 36, no. 6 (2018): 637–61.

Economist, "The Rise of the Sharing Economy," *Economist,* March 9, 2013, https://www.economist.com/news/leaders/21573104-internet-everything-hire-rise-sharing-economy.

Edwards, Allen. "The Relationship between the Judged Desirability of a Trait and the Probability That the Trait Will Be Endorsed." *Journal of Applied Psychology* 37, no. 2 (1953): 90–93.

Emerson, Robert M., Rachel I. Fretz, and Linda L. Shaw. *Writing Ethnographic Fieldnotes.* Chicago: University of Chicago Press, 1995.

Etsy. "Economic Impact of U.S. Etsy Sellers," *Etsy Dashboards.* Last updated February 27, 2019. https://dashboards.mysidewalk.com/etsy-economic-impact-1532038450.

Farnam Street. "This Is Water by David Foster Wallace (Full Transcript and Audio)." *Farnam Street,* April 2012. https://fs.blog/2012/04/david-foster-wallace-this-is-water/.

Farra, Emily. "Vegan Fashion Week Is Coming to L.A.—And It's About a Lot More Than Eco Leather and Faux Fur." *Vogue.* January 14, 2019.

https://www.vogue.com/article/vegan-fashion-week-los-angele
s-emmanuelle-rienda.

Fernback, Jan. "Beyond the Diluted Community Concept: A Symbolic
Interactionist Perspective on Online Social Relations." *New Media
and Society* 9, no. 1 (2007): 49–69.

Foertsch, Carsten. "What Is Coworking and Its Cultural Background?"
October 5, 2011. http://www.deskmag.com/en/what-is-coworkin
g-about-the-changing-labor-market-208.

Foye, Meghann. "20 Signs You Are a Xennial Working Mom." *Working
Mother*, April 2, 2018. https://www.workingmother.com/20-sign
s-you-are-xennial-working-mom.

Francisco, Eric. "New Coke Joke in 'Stranger Things' Dusts off a Soda
that Died 17 Years Ago." *Inverse*, July 3. 2019, https://www.inverse.
com/article/57348-stranger-things-season-3-new-coke-real-bri
ef-history-controversy-conspiracy.

Galindo, Brian. "60 Things You'll Only Understand if You Are a Xennial."
Buzzfeed, March 9, 2018. https://www.buzzfeed.com/briangalindo/
things-only-people-born-between-1975-1985-will-truly-get.

Gamson, William. "Review of Frame Analysis: An Essay on the
Organization of Experience by Erving Goffman." *Contemporary
Sociology* 4, no. 6 (1975): 603–7.

Garcia, Angela C., Alecea I. Standlee, Jennifer Bechkoff, and Yan
Cui. "Ethnographic Approaches to the Internet and Computer-
Mediated Communication." *Journal of Contemporary Ethnography* 38,
no. 1 (2009): 52–84.

Geertz, Clifford. "Thick Description: Toward an Interpretive Theory
of Cultures." In *The Interpretation of Cultures*, 3–30. New York: Basic
Books, 1973.

General Electric (GE) Healthcare. "From Terrifying to Terrific: The Creative Journey of the Adventure Series." September 20, 2012. http://newsroom.gehealthcare.com/from-terrifying-to-terrific-creative-journey-of-the-adventure-series/.

Gerdeman, Dina. "The Airbnb Effect: Cheaper Rooms for Travelers, Less Revenue for Hotels." *Forbes*, February 27, 2018. https://www.forbes.com/sites/hbsworkingknowledge/2018/02/27/the-airbnb-effect-cheaper-rooms-for-travelers-less-revenue-for-hotels/#7393ab92d672.

Gevelber, Lisa. "Why Consumer Intent Is More Powerful than Demographics." *Think With Google*, December 2015. https://www.thinkwithgoogle.com/marketing-resources/micro-moments/why-consumer-intent-more-powerful-than-demographics/.

Global Cosmetic Industry. "Target Manscapes Its Male Grooming Business." *Global Cosmetic Industry*, August 29, 2018. https://www.gcimagazine.com/marketstrends/consumers/men/Target-Manscapes-Its-Male-Grooming-Business—492016111.html.

Goffman, Erving. *Asylums: Essays on the Social Situation of Mental Patients and Other Inmates*. New York: Anchor Books, 1961.

Goffman, Erving. *Frame Analysis: An Essay on the Organization of Experience*. New York: Harper & Row, 1974.

Goffman, Erving. *The Presentation of Self in Everyday Life*. New York: Doubleday, 1959.

Golson, Jordan. "Well, That Didn't Work: The Segway Is a Technological Marvel. Too Bad it Doesn't Make Any Sense." *Wired*. January, 2015. https://www.wired.com/2015/01/well-didnt-work-segway-technological-marvel-bad-doesnt-make-sense/.

Goodchild, Paul. "Coworking Disrupts Office Design" *Insight*, June 10, 2019. https://workplaceinsight.net/coworking-shaping-offic e-design-ways-might-think/.

Gottschalk, Simon. "The Presentation of Avatars in Second Life: Self and Interaction in Social Virtual Spaces." *Symbolic Interaction* 33, no. 4 (2010): 501–25.

Haasch, Palmer. "New Coke is the Weirdest Pop Culture Throwback in Stranger Things 3." *Polygon*, July 6, 2019. https://www.polygon. com/2019/7/6/20683542/stranger-things-3-new-coke-198 5-coca-cola-where-to-buy.

Hancox, Dan. "The Unstoppable Rise of Veganism: How a Fringe Movement Went Mainstream." *Guardian*, April 1, 2018. https:// www.theguardian.com/lifeandstyle/2018/apr/01/vegans-ar e-coming-millennials-health-climate-change-animal-welfare.

Hansen, Robert A., and Carol A. Scott. "Alternative Approaches to Assessing the Quality of Self Report Data." In *Advances in Consumer Research*, vol. 5, edited by Kent Hunt, 99–102. Ann Arbor, MI: Association for Consumer Research, 1978.

Harris, Eli. "China's Manufacturers Are Enabling a New Model of Startup Incubation." *Venture Beat*, October 15, 2017. https:// venturebeat.com/2017/10/15/chinas-manufacturers-are-ena bling-a-new-model-of-startup-incubation/.

Harvard Health Publishing. "Should You Try the Keto Diet?" *Harvard Health Website*, October 2018. https://www.health.harvard.edu/ staying-healthy/should-you-try-the-keto-diet.

Heilemann, John. "Reinventing the Wheel." *Time*. December 2, 2001. http://www.time.com/time/business/article/0,8599,186660-1,00. html.

Henn, Steve. "What's Mine Is Yours (for a Price) in the Sharing Economy." *National Public Radio (NPR)*. November 13, 2013. https://www.npr.org/sections/alltechconsidered/2013/11/13/244860511/whats-mine-is-yours-for-a-price-in-the-sharing-economy.

Hill, Charles, Gareth Jones, and Melissa Schilling. *Strategic Management Theory: An Integrated Approach*, 11th ed. Boston, MA.: Cengage Learning, 2014.

Hine, Christine. *Virtual Ethnography.* London: Sage, 2000.

Hodson, Richard. "Special Issue: Digital Revolution." *Nature Outlook*, September 29, 2018. https://www.nature.com/articles/d41586-018-07500-z.

Howell, Ryan T. "Consumer Self-Report Data: You Can Ask What But Not Why." *Psychology Today*, November 17, 2013. https://www.psychologytoday.com/us/blog/cant-buy-happiness/201311/consumer-self-report-data-you-can-ask-what-not-why.

Howell, Ryan T. "Should Marketers Trust Consumer Self-Reports? Marketers Should Think Twice about Trusting Data from Focus Groups." *Psychology Today*, October 23, 2013. https://www.psychologytoday.com/us/blog/cant-buy-happiness/201310/should-marketers-trust-consumer-self-reports.

Huddleston Jr., Tom. "How Allbirds Went from Silicon Valley Fashion Staple to a $1.4 Billion Sneaker Start-Up." *CNBC*, December 18, 2018. https://www.cnbc.com/2018/12/14/allbirds-went-from-silicon-valley-staple-to-billion-sneaker-startup.html.

Huhtala, Hannele, and Marjo-Riitta Parzefall. "A Review of Employee Well-Being and Innovativeness: An Opportunity for a Mutual Benefit." *Creativity and Innovation Management* 16 (2007), 299–306.

IDEOU. n.d. "What Is Design Thinking?" *IDEOU* blog post, accessed June 26, 2019, https://www.ideou.com/blogs/inspiration/what-is-design -thinking.

Inside the Marketplace. "Why the Beard Grooming Market Continues to Grow." *Inside the Marketplace*, August 16, 2018. http:// insidethemarketplace.com/2018/08/16/why-the-beard-marke t-continues-to-grow/.

Jacobson, Abbi, dir. *Broad City*. Season 5, episode 2, "SheWork and S*** Bucket." Aired January 31, 2019, on HBO.

Johnson, Cat. "Look Out, Coworking. Here Comes Big Money." *Shareable*, May 13, 2016. Accessed 19 July 2019: https://www.shareable.net/ look-out-coworking-here-comes-big-money/.

Johnston, Josee, and Shyon Baumann. *Foodies: Democracy and Distinction in the Gourmet Foodscape,* 2nd ed. New York and London: Routledge, 2015.

Johnston, Josee, and Shyon Baumann. "Democracy versus Distinction: A Study of Omnivorousness in Gourmet Food Writing." *American Journal of Sociology* 113 (2007): 165–204.

Kahneman, Daniel. *Thinking Fast and Slow*. New York: Farrar, Straus and Giroux, 2011.

Kaplan, Jonas T., Sarah I. Gimbel, and Sam Harris. "Neural Correlates of Maintaining One's Political Beliefs in the Face of Counterevidence." *Scientific Reports* 6 (2016): 39589.

Kasperkevic, Jana. "Occupy Wall Street: Four Years Later." *Guardian*. September, 16, 2015. https://www.theguardian.com/world/ng- interactive/2015/sep/16/occupy-wall-street-four-years-later -timeline.

Kaysen, Ronda. "Co-Working Spaces Add a Perk for Parents: Child Care." *New York Times*, December 23, 2016. https://www.nytimes.com/2016/12/23/realestate/co-working-spaces-add-a-perk-for-parents-child-care.html.

Khan, Nahnatchka, dir. *Always Be My Maybe*. Netflix, 2019.

Kiesler, Sara, ed. *Culture of the Internet*. Mahwah, NJ: Lawrence Erlbaum, 1997.

King, Eden, Lisa Finkelstein, Courtney Thomas, and Abby Corrington. "Generational Differences at Work Are Small. Thinking They're Big Affects our Behavior." *Harvard Business Review*, August 1, 2019. https://hbr.org/2019/08/generational-differences-at-work-are-small-thinking-theyre-big-affects-our-behavior.

King, Lucy. "It's 2016 and We've Reached Peak Food Culture." *Vice*, June 27, 2016. https://www.vice.com/en_au/article/8g3mgp/its-2016-and-weve-reached-peak-food-culture.

Kolbert, Elizabeth. "Why Facts Don't Change Our Minds." *New Yorker*, February 19, 2017. https://www.newyorker.com/magazine/2017/02/27/why-facts-dont-change-our-minds.

Krajeski, Jenna. "This is Water." *New Yorker*, September 19, 2008. https://www.newyorker.com/books/page-turner/this-is-water.

Kristen Barber. *Styling Masculinity: Gender, Class, and Inequality in the Men's Grooming Industry*. New Brunswick: Rutgers University Press, 2016.

Krupnick, Matt. 2017. "Ad Campaigns Tag Along as Men Embrace Different Paths." *New York Times*, June 4, 2017. https://www.nytimes.com/2017/06/04/business/media/advertising-masculinity.html.

Kyles, Kyra. "Now Serving: Beefcake." *Chicago Tribune*, November 15, 2005. https://www.chicagotribune.com/news/ct-xpm-2005-11-15-0511150317-story.html.

Leach, Taylor. "Danone Unveils Largest Vegan Yogurt Plant in U.S." *Dairy Herd*, February 13, 2019. https://www.dairyherd.com/article/danone-unveils-largest-vegan-yogurt-plant-us.

Lebowitz, Shana, and Allana Akhtar. "There's a Term for People Born in the Early '80s who Don't Feel Like a Millennial or a Gen Xer." *Business Insider*, August 22, 2019. https://www.businessinsider.com/xennials-born-between-millennials-and-gen-x-2017-11.

Lee, Spike, dir. *When the Levees Broke: A Requiem in Four Acts*. HBO, 2006.

Li, Shan. "Vegan Fashion Grows More Fashionable as Textile Technology Improves." *Los Angeles Times*, February 4, 2015. https://www.latimes.com/business/la-fi-vegan-fashion-20150205-story.html.

Lin, Carolyn, and David Atkin, eds. *Communication, Technology and Society: New Media Adoption and Uses*. Cresskill, NJ: Hampton Press, 2002.

Linnane, Ciara. "Proctor & Gamble's Gillette Razor Business Dinged by Online Shave Clubs." *MarketWatch*, April 27, 2017. https://www.marketwatch.com/story/procter-gambles-gillette-razor-business-dinged-by-online-shave-clubs-2017-04-26.

Livingstone, Josephine. "What Was the Foodie?" *New Republic*, March 18, 2019. https://newrepublic.com/article/153335/foodie.

Lockwood, Thomas. *Design Thinking: Integrating Innovation, Customer Experience and Brand Value*. New York: Allworth, 2010.

Lohr, Steve. "IBM's Design-Centered Strategy to Set Free the Squares." *New York Times*. November 14, 2015. https://www.nytimes.com/2015/11/15/business/ibms-design-centered-strategy-to-set-free-the-squares.html.

Luenendonk, Martin. "Airbnb – Strategies for Renting Your Accomodation [*sic*] Online." *Cleverism*, November 19, 2014. https://www.cleverism.com/airbnb-strategies-selling-products-online/.

MacFadyen, Jean. "The Dance Between Innovation, Stress, and Productivity." *Holistic Nursing Practice* 29 (2015): 187–189.

Mannheim, Karl. "The Problem of Generations." In *Karl Mannheim: Essays*, edited by Paul Kecskemeti, 276–322. London: Routledge, 1952.

Mannor, Mike, Adam Wowak, Viva Ona Bartkus, and Luis R. Gomez-Mejia. "How Anxiety Affects CEO Decision Making." *Harvard Business Review*, July 19, 2016. https://hbr.org/2016/07/how-anxiety-affects-ceo-decision-making."

Marketplace. "How It Became OK for Guys to Take Care of Themselves." *Marketplace* podcast, January 6, 2016. https://www.marketplace.org/2016/01/05/world/how-it-became-ok-guys-take-care-themselves/.

MarketWatch. "Household Green Cleaning Products Market Worth $27.83 Billion by 2024 – Exclusive Report by 360iResearch." *MarketWatch*, April 24, 2019. https://www.marketwatch.com/press-release/household-green-cleaning-products-market-worth-2783-billion-by-2024-exclusive-report-by-360iresearch-2019-04-24.

Martucci, Brian. "What Is the Sharing Economy—Example Companies, Definition, Pros & Cons." *Moneycrashers*, no date, accessed July 23, 2019. https://www.moneycrashers.com/sharing-economy/.

Maule, John. "How Stress Impacts Decision Making." *Leeds University Business School Blog*, May 2, 2017. https://business.leeds.ac.uk/dir-record/research-blog/712/how-stress-impacts-decision-making.

Mazareanu, E. "Global Outsourcing Market Size 2000–2018." *Statista*, July 22, 2019. https://www.statista.com/statistics/189788/global-outsourcing-market-size/.

Mazareanu, E. "Number of Coworking Spaces in the United States from 2007 to 2022." *Statista*, August 9, 2019. https://www.statista.com/statistics/797546/number-of-coworking-spaces-us/.

Mazareanu, E. "WeWork – Statistics & Facts." *Statista*, August 13, 2019. https://www.statista.com/topics/5086/wework/.

McCann, Erin, and Anya Strzemien. "Are You Secretly a Millennial?" *New York Times*, May 14, 2019. https://www.nytimes.com/interactive/2019/05/14/style/are-you-a-millennial.html.

Meacham, Matthew, Francois Faelli, Eduardo Gimenez, and John Blasberg. "Overcoming the Existential Crisis in Consumer Goods." *Bain & Company*, March 7, 2018. https://www.bain.com/insights/overcoming-the-existential-crisis-in-consumer-goods/.

Mead, George. H. *Mind, Self, and Society: From the Standpoint of a Social Behaviorist.* Chicago: University of Chicago Press, 1934.

Mead, Rebecca. "The Airbnb Invasion of Barcelona." *The New Yorker*, April 29, 2019. https://www.newyorker.com/magazine/2019/04/29/the-airbnb-invasion-of-barcelona.

Mealey, Lorri. "A History of the Food Truck: The Rise of the Food Truck Culture. *The Balance Small Business*, last modified October 14, 2019. https://www.thebalancesmb.com/a-history-of-food-trucks-2888314.

Menand, Louis. "How Cultural Anthropologists Redefined Humanity." *New Yorker*, August 19, 2019. https://www.newyorker.com/magazine/2019/08/26/how-cultural-anthropologists-redefined-humanity.

Mims, Christoper. "Why There Are More Consumer Goods Than Ever." *Wall Street Journal*, April 25, 2016. https://www.wsj.com/articles/why-there-are-more-consumer-goods-than-ever-1461556860.

Moore, John D. "Lumbersexual Look: A Manly Guide to Rugged Style and Grooming." *Guy Counseling*, February 22, 2017. https://guycounseling.com/lumbersexual-look-style-grooming-guide/.

Nelson, Anitra. "'To Market, to Market': Eco-collaborative Housing for Sale." In *Small Is Necessary: Shared Living on a Shared Planet*, 190–213. London: Pluto Press, 2018.

Neuberg, Brad. "The Start of Coworking (from the Guy That Started It)." *Coding in Paradise* (blog), no date, accessed July 22, 2019: http://codinginparadise.org/ebooks/html/blog/start_of_coworking.html.

New Scientist. "Beliefs – Why Do We Have Them and How Did We Get Them?" *New Scientist*, April 25, 2015. https://www.scmp.com/magazines/post-magazine/article/1773296/beliefs-why-do-we-have-them-and-how-did-we-get-them.

Notable Life. "11 Signs That You're a Xennial, Not a Millennial." *Notable Life*, June 30, 2017. https://Notablelife.Com/Xennial-Millennial-Definition/.

Norton, Richie. "The 14 Most Destructive Millennial Myths Debunked by Data." *Medium*, January 19, 2017. https://medium.com/the-mission/the-14-most-destructive-millennial-myths-debunked-by-data-aa00838eecd6.

Ocejo, Richard E. *Masters of Craft: Old Jobs in the New Urban Economy*. Princeton, NJ: Princeton University Press, 2017.

Oliver, Thomas. *The Real Coke, The Real Story*. New York: Random House, 1987.

Onion, Rebecca. "Against Generations." *AEON*, May 19, 2015. https://aeon.co/essays/generational-labels-are-lazy-useless-and-just-plain-wrong.

Orbis Research. "Men's Grooming Products Market Rising Popularity in 2019, Global Insights, Key Developments of Products, Top Brands (Beiersdorf, Kroger) and Forecast Till 2023." *Reuters*, October 4, 2018. https://www.reuters.com/brandfeatures/venture-capital/article?id=56764.

Packaged Fact. "Green Cleaning Products in the U.S.," August 31, 2012. https://www.packagedfacts.com/Green-Cleaning-Products-7114196/.

Packaged Fact. "Green Household Cleaning and Laundry Products in the U.S., 3rd Edition." March 13, 2015. https://www.packagedfacts.com/Green-Household-Cleaning-8825323/.

Packer, Martin J. *The Science of Qualitative Research.* Cambridge, UK: Cambridge University Press, 2017.

Parker, Kim, and Renee Stepler. "As U.S. Marriage Rate Hovers at 50%, Education Gap in Marital Status Widens." *Pew Research Center*, September 14, 2017. https://www.pewresearch.org/fact-tank/2017/09/14/as-u-s-marriage-rate-hovers-at-50-education-gap-in-marital-status-widens/.

Parkin, Benjamin. "Barbecued Beef Heart Anyone? Offal Enjoys Its Foodie Moment." *The Wall Street Journal*, September 6, 2018. https://www.wsj.com/articles/barbecued-beef-heart-anyone-offal-enjoys-its-foodie-moment-1536243262.

Peltz, James F. "Why Americans Are Eating Less Cold Cereal for Breakfast." *Los Angeles Times*, October 10, 2016. https://www.latimes.com/business/la-fi-agenda-breakfast-cereals-20161010-snap-story.html.

Piaget, Jean. *The Origins of Intelligence in Children.* New York: International University Press, 1952.

Pithers, Ellie. "The Leather Debate: Is Vegan Leather a Sustainable Alternative to the Real Thing?" *Vogue*, April 24, 2019. https://www.vogue.co.uk/article/vegan-leather-sustainability-debate-2019.

Presi, Caterina. "Symbolic Interactionism and the Internet: The Communication of Identity in Virtual Communities of Consumption and Real Life." Paper presented at the European Marketing Academy Conference (EMAC), Glasgow, Scotland, May 2003.

Ramakrishnan, Kartik. "Global IT-BPO Outsourcing Deals Analysis." *KPMG*, May 2018. https://assets.kpmg/content/dam/kpmg/in/pdf/2018/05/KPMG-Deal-Tracker-2017.pdf.

Ramazzotti, Giorgina. "The Luxury Eco Bags That Are Good for Your Wardrobe and Your Conscience." *Vogue*, November 9, 2018. https://www.vogue.co.uk/gallery/best-eco-bags.

Ramazzotti, Giorgina. "Vegan Faux Leather Bags That Look as Good as the Real Thing." *Vogue*, November 29, 2018. https://www.vogue.co.uk/gallery/best-vegan-bags.

Ranchordás, Sofia. "Does Sharing Mean Caring? Regulating Innovation in the Sharing Economy." *Minnesota Journal of Law, Science and Technology* 16, no. 1 (2015): 413–75.

Ransby, Barbara. "Katrina, Black Women, and the Deadly Discourse on Black Poverty in America." *Du Bois Review: Social Science Research on Race* 3, no. 1 (2006): 215–22.

Rehn, Alf. "Top 5 Ways to Tackle Innovation Stress in the Workplace." *European CEO*, April 17, 2019. https://www.europeanceo.com/business-and-management/top-5-ways-to-tackle-innovation-stress-in-the-workplace/.

Robinson, Nate. "If It's Good Enough for Michael Jordan and Shaq...: Why NBA Players Love Pedicures." *Chicago Tribune*, January 15,

2019. https://www.chicagotribune.com/sports/ct-nba-player s-pedicures-20190115-story.html.

Rokka, Joonas, and Lionel Sitz. "Why Teach Ethnography to Managers (in the Big Data Era)?" *The Conversation*, October 10, 2018. https://theconversation.com/why-teach-ethnography-to-manage rs-in-the-big-data-era-104669.

Rosenbaum, Ron. "Anthony Bourdain's Theory on the Foodie Revolution." *Smithsonian*, July 14, 2014. https://www.smithsonianmag.com/arts-culture/anthony-bourdains-theory-foodie-revolution-1809 51848/.

Rothstein, Matthew. "Co-Working's Influence Is Now Everywhere in Office Space." *BISNOW*, January 8, 2018. https://www.bisnow.com/philadelphia/news/office/office-landlords-coworking-des ign-tenant-recruitment-83357.

Salpini, Cara. "Target's Goodfellow Private Label Moves into Men's Grooming." *RetailDive*, May 20, 2019. https://www.retaildive.com/news/targets-goodfellow-private-label-moves-into-mens-grooming/555145/.

Schneider, Joan, and Julie Hall. "Why Most Product Launches Fail." *Harvard Business Review*, April 2011. https://hbr.org/2011/04/why-most-product-launches-fail.

Schreiber, Tucker. "How One Couple Is Making $600,000 Per Year Selling Digital Products." *Shopify Blogs*, March 11, 2015. https://www.shopify.ca/blog/17587420-how-one-couple-is-making-600 -000-per-year-selling-digital-products.

Schwartz, Howard, and Jerry Jacobs. *Qualitative Sociology: A Method to the Madness*. New York: The Free Press, 1979.

Selye, Hans. *The Stress of Life*. New York: McGraw-Hill, 1956.

Sharlet, Jeff. "Inside Occupy Wall Street." *Rolling Stone*, November 11, 2011. https://www.rollingstone.com/politics/politics-news/inside-occupy-wall-street-236993/.

Sheth, Jagdish N. "Demographics in Consumer Behavior." *Journal of Business Research* 5 (June 1977): 129–38.

Silicon Valley Bank. "US Startup Outlook 2018: Key Insights from the Silicon Valley Bank Startup Outlook Survey." 2018. https://www.svb.com/globalassets/library/uploadedfiles/content/trends and insights/reports/startup outlook report/us/svb-suo-us-report.pdf.

Simpson, Mark. "Meet the Metrosexual: He's Well Dressed, Narcissistic and Obsessed with Butts. But Don't Call Him Gay." *Slate*, July 22, 2002. https://www.salon.com/test/2002/07/22/metrosexual/.

Sitzer, Carly. "US Milk Sales Drop by More Than $1 Billion as Plant-Based Alternatives Take Off." *World Economic Forum*, April 2, 2019. https://www.weforum.org/agenda/2019/04/milk-sales-drop-by-more-than-1-billion-as-plant-based-alternatives-take-off/.

Solomon, Steven Davidoff. "$1 Billion for Dollar Shave Club: Why Every Company Should Worry." *New York Times*, July 26, 2016. https://www.nytimes.com/2016/07/27/business/dealbook/1-billion-for-dollar-shave-club-why-every-company-should-worry.html.

St. John, Warren. "Metrosexuals Comes Out." *New York Times*, June 22, 2003. https://www.nytimes.com/2003/06/22/style/metrosexuals-come-out.html.

Stanley, Brandon. "10 Essential Features of Winning Coworking Space." *Coworker*, June 20, 2018. https://www.coworker.com/lab/10-essential-features-of-winning-coworking-space/.

Stanton, Brandon. "Adults Guess and Assume That I'm Not Going to Understand Things Just Because I'm a Little Kid." *Humans of*

New York on *Facebook*, August 6, 2019. https://www.facebook.
com/humansofnewyork/photos/a.102107073196735/33075214793
21929/?type=3&theater.

Statista Research Department. "Social Networking Time Per U.S.
User 2016, by Ethnicity." *Statista*, July 22, 2019. https://www.
statista.com/statistics/248158/social-networking-time-per-u
s-user-by-ethnicity/.

Stein, Joel. "The Me Me Me Generation: Millennials Are Lazy, Entitled
Narcissists Who Still Live with Their Parents." *Time*, May 20, 2013.
https://time.com/247/millennials-the-me-me-me-generation/.

Tabcum, Sarote Jr. "The Sharing Economy Is Still Growing, and Businesses
Should Take Note." *Forbes*, March 4, 2019. https://www.forbes.com/
sites/forbeslacouncil/2019/03/04/the-sharing-economy-is-still-
growing-and-businesses-should-take-note/#7bed100d4c33.

Talty, Alexandra. "New Study Finds Millennials Spend 44 Percent
of Food Dollars on Eating Out." *Forbes*, October 17, 2016.
https://www.forbes.com/sites/alexandratalty/2016/10/17/
millennials-spend-44-percent-of-food-dollars-on-eating-out-s
ays-food-institute/#f45a94e3ff68.

Taylor, Tegan. "Is 'Vegan Leather' a Sustainable Alternative to Animal
Leather?" *Australian Broadcasting Corporation (ABC)*, last modified
May 24, 2018, https://www.abc.net.au/news/science/2018-05-24/
vegan-leather-is-it-a-sustainable-alternative/9774768.

Thomas, William I., and Dorothy S. Thomas. *The Child in America:
Behavior Problems and Programs.* New York: Knopf, 1928.

Tiffany, Kaitlin. "The Absurd Quest to Make the 'Best' Razor." *Vox*, December
11, 2018. https://www.vox.com/the-goods/2018/12/11/18134456/
best-razor-gillette-harrys-dollar-shave-club.

TradeGecko. "How Dollar Shave Club Dominates the Cutthroat World of eCommerce." *TradeGecko*, May 22, 2018. https://www. tradegecko.com/blog/small-business-growth/how-dollar-shave -club-dominates-ecommerce.

Trafton, Anne. "Stress Can Lead to Risky Decisions." *MIT News*, November 16, 2017. http://news.mit.edu/2017/stress-can-lead-risk y-decisions-1116.

Trefis Team. "As a Rare Profitable Unicorn, Airbnb Appears to Be Worth at Least $38 Billion." *Forbes*, May 11, 2018. https://www.forbes.com/ sites/greatspeculations/2018/05/11/as-a-rare-profitable-unicor n-airbnb-appears-to-be-worth-at-least-38-billion/#148ea6452741.

Urstadt, Bryant. "Intentionally Temporary." *New York Magazine*, September 11, 2009. http://nymag.com/shopping/features/58998/.

US Census Bureau, "Geographic Area Series: Nonemployer Statistics for the US, States, Metropolitan Areas, and Counties," statistics for 2015 and 2016. *US Census Bureau*, June 21, 2018. https:// factfinder.census.gov/faces/tableservices/jsf/pages/productview. xhtml?pid=NES_2016_00A2&prodType=table.

Valenti, Lauren. "The History of Guyliner." *Marie Claire*, July 10, 2015. https://www.marieclaire.com/beauty/news/g3035/men-wearing-eyeliner-history/.

Varis, Piia. "Digital Ethnography." *Tilburg Papers in Culture Studies* 104, August 2014. https://www.tilburguniversity.edu/sites/tiu/files/ download/TPCS_104_Varis_2.pdf.

Verhaege, Annelies, Niels Schillewaert, and Emilie van den Berge. "Getting Answers without Asking Questions: The Evaluation of a TV Programme Based on Social Media." *InSites Consulting R&D White Paper Series*, 2009. https://issuu.com/insitesconsulting/docs/04_ getting_answers_without_asking_questions.

Vice Staff. "Whatever Happened to Metrosexuals?" *Vice*, June 6, 2016. https://www.vice.com/en_ca/article/3bjyek/whatever-happened-to-the-metrosexuals-324.

Wacquant, Loïc. "Pierre Bourdieu." In *Key Contemporary Thinkers*, 2nd ed., edited by Rob Stone, 261-77. Basingstoke, UK and New York: Palgrave Macmillan, 2008.

Walker, Rob. "It's a Man's World: Men's Grooming Breaks New Ground." *Global Cosmetic Industry*, February 23, 2014. https://www.gcimagazine.com/marketstrends/consumers/men/Its-a-Mans-World-Mens-Grooming-Breaks-New-Ground-246591491.html.

Walsh, Brian. "10 Ideas That Will Change the World." March 17, 2011. http://content.time.com/time/specials/packages/article/0,28804,2059521_2059717_2059710,00.html.

Wang, Tricia. "Big Data Needs Thick Data." *Ethnography Matters*, May 13, 2013. http://ethnographymatters.net/blog/2013/05/13/big-data-needs-thick-data/.

Watrous, Monika. "Coke Learns Big Lessons from Small Startups." *Food Business News*, March 18, 2016. https://www.foodbusinessnews.net/articles/7577-coke-learns-big-lessons-from-small-startups.

Watrous, Monika. "When Big Companies Buy Small Brands." *Food Business News*, March 14, 2016. https://www.foodbusinessnews.net/articles/7712-when-big-companies-buy-small-brands.

Wax, Murray L. "Paradoxes of 'Consent' to the Practice of Fieldwork." *Social Problems* 27 (1980): 272–83.

Weisenthal, Joe, and Robert Johnson. "Here's How Occupy Wall Street Came to a Sudden, Unexpected End Today." *Business Insider*, November 15, 2011. https://www.businessinsider.com/how-police-cleared-occupy-wall-street-2011-11.

Wellman, Barry, and Caroline Haythornthwaite. *The Internet in Everyday Life*. Oxford: Blackwell, 2002.

Whitehouse, John. "How Fox News Pushed Propaganda about the El Paso Mass Shooting." *Media Matters for America* (MMFA), August 4, 2019. https://www.mediamatters.org/fox-news/how-fox-new s-pushed-propaganda-about-el-paso-mass-shooting.

Wicker, Alden. "Fashion's Long Hunt for the Perfect Vegan Leather." *Vogue*, June 17, 2019. https://www.voguebusiness.com/technology/ vegan-faux-leather-stella-mccartney-prada-versace.

Williams, Alex. "'Metrosexuals' Were Just Straight Men Who Loved Self-Care. Right?" *New York Times*, June 15, 2018. https://www. nytimes.com/2018/06/15/style/metrosexuals.html.

Workman, Lance. "Daniel Kahneman on the Definition of Rationality and the Difference between Information and Insight." *The Psychologist* 22 (January 2009): 36–37. http://thepsychologist.bps. org.uk/volume-22/edition-1/most-important-living-psychologist.

Zhao, Shanyang. "The Digital Self: Through the Looking Glass of Telecopresent Others." *Symbolic Interaction* 28, no. 3 (2005): 387–405.

ABOUT THE AUTHOR

Ujwal Arkalgud is a seasoned cultural anthropologist, a pioneer in the study of culture on the Internet and CEO of MotivBase. Jason Partridge is an award-winning creative director, commercialization expert and President of MotivBase.

Over 4 years, their company has been a catalyst for corporate transformation. Their front-end innovation work has served as the building block for more than a hundred net new products and generated more than $5.9 billion in net new revenue in the consumer packaged goods, retail, beauty and beverage marketplace.

Microcultures is their follow up book to Web True.0: Why the Internet and Digital Ethnography Hold the Key to Answering the Questions that Traditional Research Just Can't.